FRANCIS
OF ASSISI

Francis
of Assisi

A Meditation on His Life and Writings

Joshua C. Benson

FOREWORD BY
Margaret Carney, OSF, STD

Paulist Press
New York / Mahwah, NJ

Library of Congress Cataloging-in-Publication Data available upon request.

ISBN 978-0-8091-5679-5 (paperback)
ISBN 978-0-8091-8849-9 (e-book)

Published by Paulist Press
997 Macarthur Boulevard
Mahwah, New Jersey 07430
www.paulistpress.com

Printed and bound in the
United States of America

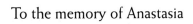

To the memory of Anastasia

Contents

Foreword

Dr. Joshua Benson attained his first degree in Franciscan studies at St. Bonaventure University. There, he walked regularly through the stacks of the Franciscan Institute's circulating collection, where space was always at a premium in the section that held books on St. Francis of Assisi. So, as he opens this small volume that he calls a "meditation," Dr. Benson reminds his readers that many will wonder why anyone would hope to create even one more volume to add to that literary cornucopia.

Benson avoids the temptation to argue his case with too many talking points. Instead, he offers the justification that a new voice, a new set of eyes, can lift from the countless pages of centuries yet another level of insight, another key to the mystery of the man from Assisi, another reason to continually turn to him as a sure guide for a Christian project of life.

The work you now begin to read is more than ample proof that Benson has given us just such a new way of meditating on the core meanings of the writings of Francis of Assisi. He has also brought into the witness box, so to speak, precious citations from the earliest biographies of the saint to help us see what the contemporaries of Francis saw and described. In other words, how they saw the intentions of Francis become incarnated on a daily basis. This meditation book is focused on the most basic primary sources that contain the original inspiration of this saint. Until recently, these sources were restricted to an academic audience skilled in Latin and the use of the historical-critical method. The works on St. Francis based on such materials rarely made it into general circulation. Add to this the fact that a type of folklore (*The Little Flowers of St. Francis*) with Francis as its subject was one of the very popular ancient sources that did manage to find a large audience over the centuries. Thus, it was a Francis of story, song, symbol, and cinema that drew many to appreciate and revere him.

Joshua Benson has undertaken the task of plumbing the depths of the writings by and about Francis with all the academic skill described above. However, he is not trying to advance a scholarly argument or display his very substantial expertise. He comes to this task as a fellow pilgrim. Yes, he has been associated with some of the most important translations and academic publications of recent times relating to St. Francis, but he turns now to the reader in a fraternal stance to open and share the treasury of personal inspiration and enlightenment that this work has afforded him.

What is so appealing about this meditation is the flow of the author's movement from initial concepts and interpretations to the gradual uncovering of layers of meaning drawn from a deeper well of insight. The waters of that well are fed by two powerful streams: a commitment to exacting scholarship and a personal desire to appropriate the fruit of such study.

Benson allows us to share his own meditation on the Scriptures—what he calls the "Letter," which became the sole guide for Francis's way of following Jesus Christ. By using the device of "the Letter," he continually takes us to new lights appearing on the Franciscan path. He is also able to use this centrality of the Letter in multivalent ways bringing us to appreciate the deep coherence in which the life of Francis unfolded. We cannot avoid the conclusion that what matters most in the mind of Francis is the determination to take the Gospel seriously and to make of it a pattern for life, a pattern that mirrors the life of Jesus of Nazareth. In the end, that alone matters.

Another appealing feature of this work is Benson's ability to contextualize details with helpful explanations of their medieval origins or meanings. This prevents us from missing some of the poetry and drama that a modern reader would not discover without such help. A good example is found in the sixth chapter, where he describes the reconciliation of Assisi's mayor and bishop in response to the message Francis embedded in his "Canticle of the Sun." (The friars summoned the two leaders who were embroiled in mutual hatreds to hear the song as a special plea for mutual forgiveness from the dying saint.) In recalling that somber day in Assisi's history, Benson takes the time to teach us about the rituals of medieval contractual relationships that were being enacted. In other words, the narrative we have is not simply telling a good story, it contains details that assure us that these two powerful men made a formal and intentional new pact witnessed by many citizens. Such guidance is found in multiple instances, but it never feels like distracting pedantry.

The text weaves threads of hagiography, linguistics, theology, study of the Scriptures, and history into a unified whole, a veritable feast of beautifully crafted interpretive reflections. These carry us into the spirit that Benson remembers experiencing when he visited Assisi and knew in his own mind and heart its special peace, its unique atmosphere of spiritual energies.

Nor is the meditation a nostalgic exercise in calling up memories of long-ago holiness and devotional life. The continual emphasis on the central lines of the faith and love of Francis leads us to reflect on how those realities of loving faith are available through the Spirit's action in our own time and place—the Eucharist as the continuing presence of Jesus in our lives, a prayer life clearly immersed in the Scriptures through the Divine Office, the determination to live in humility and simplicity as a personal response to the Gospel's call, the refusal to shrink from suffering and to find in it a path of closeness to the Crucified One, the mystical insight that we are related intimately to all of creation as children of one creating God. These central commitments of an evangelical life are made possible because of the never-failing overshadowing of the Holy Spirit. The same Spirit that moved Francis seeks to move us as well. Too many admirers of the *Poverello* feel incapable of adopting even a small part of his brave Christian dedication. The lack of confidence that the Spirit is also present in each age, to each of us, keeps Francis on a pedestal and us the poorer for that perception of him as a distant and detached ascetic hero.

Finally, an element of welcome newness courses through the text. Benson comes to this meditation as a lay theologian, husband, and father. This human reality of his life grounds his experience and admiration. He sees and emphasizes the way in which Francis moves to deeper understanding of his call through the physical world, through his own body, and through the people who make up his expanding community of sisters and brothers. While this insight is quietly tucked into multiple parts of the meditation, it rises as a refrain that reminds us over and over that we are dealing with a saint who did not fear the physical world but saw it in the glorious light of Creation when God declared that all was good. That very word is then given back over and over as the definition of God's nature: overflowing goodness.

I welcome this new and thoroughly inviting reflection. I hope that for many it brings Francis closer as one who can befriend us as we grow in our understanding of his amazing experience of the Letter and the Spirit. Now Francis is sharing that through the work that Joshua Benson created with such refined insight. He brings to our twenty-first-century minds a loving appreciation of the man known in ages past as the Mirror of Christ. May its mission be fulfilled with each person who spends time being taught and encouraged by these meditations.

Margaret Carney, OSF, STD
President Emeritus, St. Bonaventure University

Preface

Reminders of St. Francis surround us in books and films, in churches and in gardens, yet we never tire of him. We want to hear how he followed the Lord without reserve because we know we must hear it again and again until we begin to do it ourselves. We read about the saints because we love what is good. Their lives seem almost reckless, passionate to a fault, but what a happy fault to spend your life totally for another, totally for God in whom all good rests.

But "is there anything new under [Brother] Sun" about St. Francis (see Eccl 1:9)? Fortunately, new historical data about Francis is discovered and interpreted every year. A newly discovered medieval life of Francis was recently published, and even more recently scholars discovered a sermon on the Our Father that Francis may have authored.[1] We welcome the new information because we hope it will refresh our understanding. New data, though, is not the only way to enliven our minds. The book you hold is an attempt to remember Francis anew by giving an important place to Francis's writings, especially on the Eucharist. Francis wrote

---

1. The "new" life is translated in Jacques Dalarun, *The Rediscovered Life of St. Francis of Assisi*, trans. Timothy J. Johnson (St. Bonaventure, NY: Franciscan Institute Publications, 2016). The text on the Our Father appears in François d'Assise, *Commentaire du Notre Père, un document inconnu du Poverello?*, ed. and trans. Dominique Poirel (Paris: Les Éditions du Cerf, 2019).

about the Eucharist often, and his insight into this sacrament of memory helps us understand much of what he wrote, what he did, and what happened to him. The connection between Francis's life and writings and his eucharistic piety becomes clearer if we recognize that the Eucharist displays a pattern central to understanding the Christian mystery: the pattern of Letter and Spirit.

"Letter and Spirit" relates to an ancient and medieval way to think of Sacred Scripture as possessing a literal and a spiritual meaning. "Letter," therefore, encompasses first the words of Sacred Scripture and the words of rituals that rely upon the Scriptures. By extension, all the details of our life and the created world can also be viewed as Letters God has given us. The Spirit enables us to see more in all these Letters—these basic facts, expressions, and realities—these gifts. Through the Spirit, we see the living God who has given us these Letters and who gave his life for us, we see the life to which God now calls us, and we see something of the life we hope to have eternally with God and how we can approach that life now. This interaction of Letter and Spirit is seen clearly in the sacraments, for in the sacraments we say the letters, the words of a ritual, and the Spirit comes to transform. Francis himself once reflected on the pattern of Letter and Spirit. His words come at this mystery from a different angle but can still illuminate our meditation. In the Admonitions (Adm VII), Francis took as his starting point Paul's famous phrase regarding the relationship between the old and new covenants: "the letter kills, but the Spirit gives life" (2 Cor 3:6). For Francis, we are killed by the letter when we only want to know the words of the Scriptures for our own glory and wish to claim what belongs to God as our own. In contrast, we are brought to life by the Spirit when "by word and example" we return the Letters we have come to know "to the Most High Lord God to Whom every good belongs" (Adm VII, 4). When we return to God the good that God gives to us, more always happens. In Francis's own life, he certainly attempted to return all that God gave him by word and example. He lived his life as close to the Letter of the Gospel as he could, and the Spirit worked through him and in him. He also recognized that the Letter of creation could be seen with the Spirit's power, so that creation communicated now dimly, now brilliantly, the presence of the God who made and sustains it. "Letter and Spirit," then, is a theme that we can use to aid our meditation on what Francis wrote and what he did. Letter and Spirit can also help us understand the mystery at the end of Francis's life, which is always in need of fresh understanding—the mystery of the stigmata.

Francis of Assisi heard and responded to the call of God and was transformed in his mind and memory, his prayer, his activity, and his very body. But rather than meditate on Francis and his transformation, we more often dote on the memory of a man who danced in fields and played in the sun, who talked to birds and wolves, whose statue can be safely kept in our gardens. Musing on this innocent simpleton, we may wonder how he could also be the man who miraculously bore the wounds of Christ. The two images of Francis seem incongruous: the gladsome fool and the gruesome penitent. We therefore reject one image and keep the other, clinging to our laughing hippy or our stigmatic mystic, perhaps because we hope to be one of these but not the other. We must form our memories differently.

When we remember the lives of the saints, the memories stir us because of what happened in and through them. In the telling of their stories, the Eternal Father, who desires our memory, calls to us. The Eternal Father desires not just a receptacle of facts but the whole of our memory. He desires the root of our soul, which he has planted. Through the pattern of Letter and Spirit, God calls to our memory in the Letter of creation, where "through the things he has made," we are led to the invisible Creator of them all (Rom 1:20). God calls to us in worship, especially through the Letter of Scripture, the record of God's love for us, which sharpens our vision of creation's purpose. God calls to us in the Eucharist, where through the Son's own words and the power of the Spirit, our gifts become the Son's body and blood. In the Eucharist we cannot fail to recall the Lord's sacrifice, his resurrection, and the power of the Spirit who draws us into one body as we consume the body in which we are one.

But why does it matter that we remember the saints? In the stories of the saints lie the power of transformation. The history of the saints is the history of the Spirit's work to bring all things through Christ to God the Father. If we fail to remember the saints, we think less of the Spirit's work and its possibilities. We forget that the Lord can be followed. We forget the Father's voice.

Wishing to remember Francis better, I have written the seven chapters that follow. Although I am confident that the life and writings of Francis of Assisi can display much about Christian transformation, I know that my telling of it may fail because my own transformation is so deeply incomplete. I also know that any transformation in the reader depends, too, on the reader's openness and on the grace of God. Let us together pray for the grace of transformation from the God who grants it as we can remember what God had done in the saints, especially in St. Francis of Assisi.

A NOTE ON TEXTS

Throughout this book I will use (with modification) the English translations published in the series *Francis of Assisi Early Documents*, 3 vols., ed. Regis J. Armstrong, OFM Cap;

Preface

J. A. Wayne Hellmann, OFM Con; and William J. Short, OFM (New York: New City Press, 1999–2001). I have also used sources related to Clare of Assisi. The interested reader can find many of these texts on the website franciscantradition .org. Membership is free and allows access to English and Latin texts. I will employ the abbreviations used by the *Francis of Assisi: Early Documents* series when I cite the texts of Francis or the medieval texts about him, followed by the paragraph or line number in these volumes. I list the abbreviations below. Because these paragraph divisions are taken from the standard Latin editions and are replicated in most translations, readers should be able to find a reference no matter what translation they use. I also cite from a recently discovered life of Francis by Thomas of Celano. I note this text below and create an abbreviation for it. I reference the text according to the paragraph numbers that correspond to both the English translation and the Latin edition. For the Latin of Francis's writings, I have used: Carlo Paolazzi, *Francisci Assisiensis Scripta, Spicilegium Bonaventurianum* 36 (Grottaferrata, Rome: Editiones Collegii S. Bonaventurae ad Claras Aquas, 2009). For the medieval sources on Francis's life, I have often used the original published edition, though my references agree with the convenient collection *Fontes Franciscani*, ed. Enrico Menestò (Assisi: Edizioni Porziuncula, 1995). Note that for those wishing to consult the manuscript information and variants for any of these sources, the original edition (noted in the *Fontes*) must be obtained. I have also utilized a work to understand Francis's Office of the Passion better and because I cite it in this meditation, I give it an abbreviation as well.

Readers who have further interest in the life of Francis can consult many books of which I list a few of the more accessible here. I am indebted to all these presentations of Francis but to keep this work mostly free of notes I have not continually referenced them: Lawrence S. Cunningham, *Francis of Assisi: Performing the Gospel Life* (Grand Rapids: Eerdmans, 2004); Chiara Frugoni, *Francis of Assisi*, trans. John Bowden (New York: Continuum, 1998); Raoul Manselli, *St. Francis of Assisi*, trans. Paul Duggan (Chicago: Franciscan Herald Press, 1988); Augustine Thompson, *Francis of Assisi: A New Biography* (Cornell, NY: Cornell University Press, 2012); and André Vauchez, *Francis of Assisi: The Life and Afterlife of a Medieval Saint*, trans. Michael F. Cusato (New Haven, CT: Yale University Press, 2012).

For more specific information on the writings of Francis see the following very helpful volumes: *Studies in Early Franciscan Sources*, ed. Michael W. Blastic, OFM; Jay M. Hammond; and J. A. Wayne Hellmann, OFM Conv. Vol. 1, *The Writings of Francis of Assisi: Letters and Prayers*; Vol. 2, *The Writings of Francis of Assisi: Rules, Testament and Admonitions* (St. Bonaventure, NY: Franciscan Institute Publications, 2011). There are at least two useful book-length treatments of Francis's Canticle of Creatures (also known as the Canticle of Brother Sun) that have also aided my reflections: Jacques Dalarun, *The Canticle of Brother Sun: Francis of Assisi Reconciled*, trans. Philippe Yates (St. Bonaventure, NY: Franciscan Institute Publications, 2016) and Brian Moloney, *Francis of Assisi and His "Canticle of Brother Sun" Reassessed* (New York: Palgrave MacMillan, 2013).

For a brief history of the Franciscan order, see Dominic Monti, *Francis and His Brothers: A Popular History of the Franciscan Friars* (Cincinnati: St. Anthony Messenger Press, 2009).

Acknowledgments

This book began over ten years ago. I gave a "transitus" address for Francis's feast in 2012 that was published later in the *Cord* 63, no. 1 (2013): 27–35, with the title "Hold Back Nothing for Yourselves." I received positive thoughts on that address, which pushed me toward this book. I have taught many classes touching on Francis and Clare at The Catholic University of America, and when I was a professor at St. Bonaventure University between 2018 and 2020, I taught the core class on Francis and Clare consistently. Teaching those students helped me further develop these reflections. I am grateful to them and many other students at St. Bonaventure and CUA. I am especially grateful to people who read drafts of this text and who gave me so much encouragement (and criticism): Brad, Chad, Frank, Hugh, Vincent, Kathleen, Mark, Nancy, Nicholas, Tommy, Trevor, and others. I am also grateful to my editor at Paulist Mary Dern Walker. Many thanks also go to Sr. Margaret Carney, OSF, for writing the foreword. She has been an aid to me and my family for many years, not least when she was the director of the Franciscan Institute. I am also grateful to my wife, Shari, for allowing me time to work. She runs our home with amazing efficiency and love. Finally, I am grateful to Jerry, pilgrim traveler; this book would not have been possible without him.

Abbreviations

GENERAL

CA:ED   *Clare of Assisi: Early Documents, The Lady*, ed. and trans. Regis J. Armstrong (New York: New City Press, 2006)

FA:ED 1   *Francis of Assisi: Early Documents*, vol. 1, *The Saint*, ed. Regis J. Armstrong, OFM Cap; J. A. Wayne Hellmann, OFM Conv; and William J. Short, OFM (New York: New City Press, 1999)

FA:ED 2   *Francis of Assisi: Early Documents*, vol. 2, *The Founder*, ed. Regis J. Armstrong, OFM Cap; J. A. Wayne Hellmann, OFM Conv; and William J. Short, OFM (New York: New City Press, 2000)

WRITINGS OF FRANCIS

1LtCus   "The First Letter to the Custodians" (*FA:ED* 1:56–57)

2LtF   "Later Admonition and Exhortation to the Brothers and Sisters of Penance" or "Second Version of the Letter to the Faithful" (*FA:ED* 1:45–51)

Adm   "The Admonitions" (*FA:ED* 1:128–137)

CtC	"The Canticle of Creatures," "Canticle of Brother Sun" (*FA:ED* 1:113–14)
ER	Earlier Rule (Rule without a Papal Seal)
GOfP	*The Geste of the Great King: Office of the Passion of Francis of Assisi,* Laurent Gallant and André Cirino (St. Bonaventure, NY: The Franciscan Institute, 2001)
LtAnt	"A Letter to Brother Anthony of Padua" (*FA:ED* 1:107)
LtOrd	"A Letter to the Entire Order" (*FA:ED* 1:116–121)
LtR	"A Letter to the Rulers of the Peoples" (*FA:ED* 1:58–59)
OfP	The Office of the Passion (*FA:ED* 1:139–157)
PrCr	"The Prayer before the Crucifix" (*FA:ED* 1:40)
PrH	"The Praises to be Said at All the Hours" (*FA:ED* 1:161–62)
PrOF	"A Prayer Inspired by the Our Father" (*FA:ED* 1:158–59)
PrsG	"The Praises of God" (*FA:ED* 1:109)
RH	A Rule for Hermitages (*FA:ED* 1:61–62)
SalBVM	"A Salutation of the Blessed Virgin Mary (*FA:ED* 1:163)
Test	*The Testament* (*FA:ED* 1:124–27)

EARLY SOURCES

1C	*The Life of Saint Francis,* Thomas of Celano (*FA:ED* 1:180–308)
2C	*The Remembrance of the Desire of a Soul,* Thomas of Celano (*FA:ED* 2:239–398)
AC	*Assisi Compilation* (*FA:ED* 2:113–230)

Abbreviations

L3C	*Legend of the Three Companions* (*FA:ED* 2:61–110)
PC	*The Acts of the Process of Canonization* (of St. Clare) (*CA:ED* 139–96)
RL	*The Rediscovered Life of St. Francis of Assisi,* trans. Timothy J. Johnson (St. Bonaventure, NY: Franciscan Institute Publications, 2016)

1

Testament/*Testamentum*

Francis loved mountain heights. Many of the hermitages he cherished can still be visited: the Carceri above Assisi, Monte Casale near Arrezo, the more famous La Verna, and many others. Francis also used to visit a simple hermitage outside the city walls of Cortona called "Le Celle." Now the cells of Le Celle crowd along the hillside like a busy honeycomb of roofs and windows. A brook flows past the cells, giving a peaceful rhythm to the quiet.

Francis visited Le Celle more than once. His final visit came in 1225 or 1226 as he was on his way to Assisi and his death. He was very sick. His eyes perhaps caused him the most suffering, constantly filling with fluid and ringing with pain in the presence of light. In a small room, which you can still visit, he slept with his companions, he prayed near the gentle brook, and he may have begun musing about an admonition to all his brothers, his *Testament*. In this brief text Francis combines personal remembrances of his life with counsels of an almost legal character about how to observe the Rule and life of the brotherhood. In fact, toward the end of the *Testament*, Francis admonishes the brotherhood that when the Rule of the order is read at their triannual meetings (called "chapters"), the *Testament* should also be read (*Test* 37). Still, Francis denies that the *Testament* is another rule. He asserts, instead, that the text is a "remembrance, admonition, exhortation, and my testament" (*Test* 34). The *Testament* is a text of memory, guided by a litany of persons and places. If we follow this litany, we can orient ourselves to some events in Francis's life and how he perceived his life. Francis's text of memory begins as follows:

> The Lord gave me, Brother Francis, thus to begin doing penance in this way: for when I was in sin, it seemed too bitter for me to see lepers. And the Lord Himself led me among them and I showed mercy to them. And when I left them, what had seemed bitter to me was turned into sweetness of soul and body. And afterwards I delayed a little and left the age [*saeculo*]. (*Test* 1–3)

Francis's memories begin with ringing change, responding to the Lord's prompting and an outcast body: the leper. Before we consider further who these lepers were, we should briefly recall who Francis was when he was led among them.

Francis was born sometime in 1182 in Assisi, a small Italian town. His father, Pietro, was a successful cloth merchant; his mother was named Pica. Francis had at least one sibling, a brother named Angelo, who eventually took up his father's business. The family was well-off. As a boy, Francis received some formal education in grammar and perhaps mathematics. He learned French. When he was ready to work with his father, Francis displayed his natural generosity, giving away money and other things to the poor of Assisi. Francis was well-known to his fellow citizens. He was friendly and enjoyed life. He partied but wasn't excessive. He was showy but not a show-off.

This didn't seem like enough, however. Francis wanted more. He was not content with simply following the family business and being a cloth merchant like his father. His heart was restless; St. Augustine might have told him it was not yet resting in the Lord. While growing up, Francis had absorbed popular stories of chivalry and courtly love. So, he decided that the "more" he desired was to become a knight, and his parents obliged. Francis, who would later become known as a peacemaker, trained in war and prepared for battle, not out of thirst for blood, but thirst for glory, thirst for more. Around the year 1202, he fought for Assisi against archrival Perugia. Assisi lost. Francis became a prisoner of war for about a year. His father eventually paid the ransom and freed his son. Some of the medieval sources relate that while Francis was imprisoned, he retained his basically serene attitude toward life. When a fellow prisoner berated Francis for being cheerful in prison, Francis said, "What do you think will become of me? I will yet be revered [*adhuc adorabor*] throughout the whole world" (L3C 2).

Even imprisonment did not deter Francis's desire to be a knight. After his release, Francis again sought out the glory of arms. This time he was turned aside by dreams and a voice, reported in various sources. In one version, Francis explained during a dream his plan to become a knight in Apulia. A voice responded, "'Who can do more for you, the servant or the lord?' 'The Lord,' said Francis. 'Then why do you seek the servant instead of the Lord?' Francis then asked: 'Lord, what do you want me to do?' And the Lord said to him: 'Go back to the land of your birth because I will fulfill your dream in a spiritual way'" (2C 6).

Francis's simple response to the new movement in his life ("what do you want me to do?") soon had an effect. Parties

3

and late nights lost their savor. He began to frequent secluded places outside of Assisi's walls for prayer. He hung out in abandoned churches and worked on them. He wept. Soon those close to him did not understand him, especially his father. Concerned over how Francis's actions might impact the family business, his father sought him out, dragged him home and bound him, only to have Pica set her son free. Pietro had recourse to the law. The family ended up in the square before the bishop's residence, where father and son parted company for good when Francis publicly renounced his father, his inheritance, and all that he owned and stripped himself naked. The bishop covered him with a cloak, a comforting and symbolic gesture. Francis was leaving "the age."

With this bare outline of Francis's early life in view, it may not seem so strange to us, though it was surprising to him, that around 1205 he was led among the lepers, among outcasts, among rejected, diseased bodies. Lepers in the Middle Ages could be any person with a disfiguring disease. True outcasts, they lived on the fringes of cities and towns in *leprosaria*, leper colonies, where they may or may not have received much care. They were not welcome in Assisi. With the sure knowledge that a similar plight could befall the caretaker, to be among them was an act of extraordinary charity. But then one day, Francis was able to move past those cares and embrace the face of someone whose very appearance had repulsed him before. He did not do this by himself. He followed the prompting of the Lord who led him. The Lord who works changes in all things changed Francis through the broken bodies, making sweet what had been bitter, not just for the soul but the body too, for the Lord who took our nature upon himself transforms the whole of our nature. The mercy Francis showed in turn became a mercy received, an exchange that was not an end but a beginning.

From one abandoned body Francis was led to another. The *Testament* continues:

> And the Lord gave me such faith in churches that I would pray with simplicity in this way and say: "We adore you, Lord Jesus Christ, in all our Churches throughout the whole world and we bless you because by your holy cross You have redeemed the world." (*Test* 4–5)

The churches Francis has in mind were the physical spaces he began to frequent and repair in the years around 1205: the churches of San Damiano and St. Mary of the Angels, also known as the Portiuncula. These old churches, outside the city walls of Assisi, had fallen into disuse. In the dank shadows of these rundown spaces, Francis worked and prayed. The prayer he remembers saying springs from the liturgy, from the spiritual bosom of the physical spaces he worked to repair. The focus of his prayer was on the presence of Christ in those spaces and the healing power of the cross. If we concentrate on Francis's focus in the *Testament*, we see how deeply physical his spirituality is. Francis's faith in churches is not faith in an abstraction, but rather faith inspired by a physical space that can mediate the sacred, whose broken stones needed mending just like lepers' bodies needed cleansing. As we shall see in different ways, Francis's rigorous simplicity challenges us to concentrate upon precisely what is in front of us, for the things of the world that we can see and touch are a gateway to the God who in divine simplicity cannot be seen or touched.

In the space of the church, echoing with his praise and the work of his hands, Francis meets the priest and the body he administers, the Eucharist, and the words that allow him to do so, the Scriptures. The *Testament* continues:

5

Afterwards the Lord gave me, and gives me still, such faith in priests who live according to the rite of the holy Roman church because of their orders that, were they to persecute me, I would still want to have recourse to them. And if I had as much wisdom as Solomon and found impoverished priests of this age [*saeculi*], I would not preach in their parishes against their will. And I desire to respect, love and honor them and all others as my lords. And I do not want to consider any sin in them because I discern the Son of God in them and they are my lords. And I act in this way because, in this age [*saeculo*], I see nothing corporally of the most high Son of God except his most holy Body and Blood which they receive and they alone administer to others. I want to have these most holy mysteries honored and venerated above all things and I want to reserve them in precious places. Wherever I find our Lord's most holy names and words in unbecoming places, I want to gather them up and I beg that they be gathered up and placed in a becoming place. (*Test* 6–12)

Faith in priests. If we have rosy visions of the Middle Ages as an age of faith in which all priests were saints and all laypeople haloed servants, we are mistaken. To express faith in priests then was not different than expressing faith in priests now: we are expressing faith in people, people whom God has called to his service, but people, nonetheless. The scandals of our day seem to make Francis's commitment to priests naive to a fault. A few words from Francis's "Admonitions" can contextualize his commitment. In Admonition 3 Francis commends total obedience to one's superior, or prelate, but then adds the qualification that "if the prelate commands something contrary to his [that is, the subordinate's] conscience, even though he may not obey him, let him not however, abandon him" (Adm 3.7). Though this counsel may go down more easily than that of the *Testament*, it also demands more of us than just the refusal to obey. Our disobedience must be discerning, and we must be ready to aid appropriately even those whom we cannot follow.

Rather than focus on the dissonance we may perceive between Francis and ourselves, we should focus on the reason he venerates priests: they administer the body and blood of the Lord, a mystery brought about through Letter and Spirit. Francis's deeply physical, literal vision of Christian life emerges here fully, as he reminds us that the body and blood of the Lord are the only things we see physically, bodily, of Christ in this life. Francis therefore venerates and wishes to be obedient to the sacred office of the priesthood, to serve it. But we should take notice: Francis understands that the mystery the priest holds is one the priest receives and administers. The priest does not own the mystery of the Lord's body and blood; he does not make the mystery. His sacred task is to receive and give the mystery to others, to pronounce the Letters upon which the Spirit alights to make Christ present. Francis stands in awe of this sacred ministry.

The mystery that the priest administers must also be kept in precious places. We rightly associate Francis with poverty, but Francis would not have the body and blood of the Lord treated poorly. A church that lacks beauty and liturgical vessels that do not shine with purpose cannot remind our scattered minds that here in church, they must be focused on the body and blood of the Lord. For, this is the body that has saved us, remade us, and into whose likeness we hope to be transformed. For the same reason, the names and words of the Lord must also be kept in precious places. The words of the Lord are Letters brimming with the

Spirit's power to change bread into Christ's body, wine into his blood, the sinner into a reconciled brother, the soul burdened with original sin into one washed clean. In some of the stories about Francis, he goes even further, wishing that any writing at all be picked up and held in a precious place, even the writings of the pagans, "because they have the letters which make up the glorious name of the Lord God. And the good that is found there does not belong to the pagans nor to any human being, but to God alone 'to whom belongs every good thing'" (1C 82). Letters, actual written letters, as many scholars have pointed out, have a sacramental character for Francis. As "sacraments," Francis knows letters come alive when they are consumed by the mind and heart and stored in the memory to be meditated upon by human beings whose lives can become conformed by the Spirit to Christ, poor and crucified (2C 105).

Francis's focus on the words, the letters that bring change, leads him to those that work with letters. "And we must honor," he continues in the *Testament*, "all theologians and those who minister the most holy divine words and respect them as those who minister to us *spirit and life*" (John 6:63; *Test* 13). There is undoubtedly much hiding behind these words because the acquisition of learning was a contested matter within the Order of Friars Minor, the true name of the Order we call the Franciscans. Francis himself thought that learning should not be sought by those in the order who did not already have it. St. Anthony, a trained theologian and preacher, caused some concern when he joined the brotherhood because of his learning. Francis responded in a letter stating, "I am pleased that you teach sacred theology to the brothers providing that, as is contained in the Rule, you 'do not extinguish the Spirit of prayer and devotion,' during study of this kind" (LtAnt 2). Theology could be good honest work that opened into prayer and so had a place in the order. In the *Testament*, which is later than the letter to Anthony, Francis takes another strategy. Much as he had with the priest, Francis directs us to the theologian's purpose: to expound the Lord's words. To see the force of this, we should reflect on who theologians were at this point in history.

Theologians were perhaps the most learned people in the Middle Ages. At that time, a university-trained theologian first had to acquire education in the seven liberal arts, which by Francis's time were becoming more and more associated with the disciplines of logic and natural philosophy. This could require at least six years of detailed textual study. Training in theology took at least a further six years of focused study on the Bible and Peter Lombard's *Sentences*. Peter Lombard was himself a university-trained theologian and eventually bishop of Paris before he died in 1160. The *Sentences* were an ordered treatment of the many topics in theology beginning with understanding the Trinity, then creation, sin, the incarnation, virtues, sacraments, and last things (heaven, hell, judgment). The medieval "Master of Theology" (our PhD) then had a series of tasks: to lecture on the Scriptures, to train students through the public exercise of asking theological questions, and to preach.

Of course, these extraordinarily learned men were the ones chosen for further positions of authority within the Church and the broader society. Francis rightly had concerns about learning since learning meant power and influence, something he had left behind for the poverty of the Gospel. But just as Francis understood with the priest in the *Testament*, so Francis understands that the task of the theologian is not to hoard, but to spread the Lord's own words, which according to John 6:63 are "spirit and life." Francis's perspective places the theologian in a place of humble service and ministry, not lordship or ownership. Whatever power or authority society may wish to give the theologian (or any learned person), Francis calls the theologian back to the essential task of preaching the Lord's words to those who have not heard or understood them.

Francis now moves in his *Testament* to the brotherhood:

> And after the Lord gave me some brothers, no one showed me what I had to do, but the Most High Himself revealed to me that I should live according to the pattern of the Holy Gospel. And I had this written down simply and in a few words and the Lord Pope confirmed it for me. And those who came to receive life gave whatever they had to the poor and were content with one tunic, patched inside and out, with a cord and short trousers. We desired nothing more...and we were unimportant [*idiotae*] and subject to all. (*Test* 14–17, 19)

Led by the Lord among broken lepers, into crumbling churches, to forgotten priests, to the Lord's own body and blood and the Words of God that enable that mystery, and to theologians, Francis is now led among brothers, gifted to him by the Lord. When they come, he is led again to the Word of God, to the Gospel, to this Letter as the pattern of their life. The advent of brothers also leads Francis back to the space of the Church and the priest, to Rome and the pope, for confirmation of his Gospel pattern. What the brothers come to receive is not viewed simply as a religious rule to be followed but as life itself gifted from the one who is Life.

Early brothers, like the wealthy Bernard, the simple mystic Giles, and the priest Sylvester, sought out Francis because they wanted to embrace the life he had embraced. These very different men desired the risk of the Gospel and the simplicity and poverty Francis had found in leaving the age behind. Bernard was from Assisi and had seen Francis parading around town in gaudy clothes made of expensive cloth. Now Bernard saw Francis walking those same streets in a rough, patched tunic, preaching the Gospel, begging for food, working his hands to the bone, growing in a joy that came from a source he couldn't see. The change in Francis's life was evident and magnetic. The magnetism those early brothers and sisters (like Clare of Assisi) sensed was not just Francis but the Letter of the Gospel, through which the Spirit radiated and gave strength to endure joyfully all that would come.

2

The Most Holy Body and Blood of the Lord/
Sanctissimum corpus et sanguis Domini

For I received from the Lord what I also handed on to you, that the Lord Jesus on the night when he was betrayed took a loaf of bread, and when he had given thanks, he broke it and said, "This is my body that is for you. Do this in remembrance of me." In the same way he took the cup also, after supper, saying, "This cup is the new covenant in my blood. Do this, as often as you drink it, in remembrance of me." For as often as you eat this bread and drink the cup, you proclaim the Lord's death until he comes. (1 Cor 11:23–26)

Baptism and Eucharist. The Church follows the Lord's words with regard to these two sacraments as closely as possible.

Jesus told the apostles to baptize all nations in the name of the Father, the Son, and the Holy Spirit (Matt 28:19). The Church does this. The liturgy of baptism is longer, but at base the Church does what Jesus asks and keeps doing it. The same is true of the Eucharist. The Church does what Christ asked, as St. Paul witnesses in his First Letter to the Corinthians. Of course, daily liturgies and Sunday liturgies are longer than the time it takes to say these words because these words, of such power, need a prelude, instruction, praise, and absorption. However, the Church says the words and knows in faith that when it says them, the Lord will be present, the Lord will feed his people, the Lord will unite his people by the power of his Spirit and offer them to the Father through the offering of himself. Without the Letters of the Lord, without the pronouncement of these very words, the Spirit will not come, no change will be wrought in the gifts we bring, nor in our bodies and souls. Letter and Spirit. Say the Letter, and the Spirit will come. Observe the Letter and see what the Spirit does.

As Paul's words make clear, we must remember to offer the bread and wine, the body and blood. So, we make calendars to remember it, keep books to help us remember, and set aside places in which to remember it. When we go to church, we must further remember to receive well the memory that is coming at the liturgy: the memory of the Lord himself, the memory of the one who is so powerful that whenever we gather in his name to remember, he is there (Matt 18:20).

Francis's writings are razor sharp when it comes to the memory of the Lord in the Eucharist. He chides us to remember the simplest features of the Eucharist and their significance. Through Francis's words, the liturgy becomes a school of humility and charity and the Lord himself our teacher. It is not just knowledge, however, that the Lord transmits to us in worship but life, flowing from the love he bears us. The significance of the body and blood of the Lord is such a major feature of Francis's texts that I will select just a few passages. We can begin with Francis's searing "Letter to the Entire Order," written about 1225.

Scholars believe Francis composed this letter because of a 1224 papal document that gave the order permission to celebrate liturgies in their own churches. Whatever the reason, Francis challenges everyone in the order, especially priests, to observe the liturgy and all things associated with it as strictly and reverently as possible. Some of the themes of this letter are also in the *Testament*: deep reverence for priests because of their ministry, concern for fitting and well-cared for liturgical vessels and liturgical books, and a concern for the very words that bring about the sacrament, "For many things are made holy by the words of God and the sacrament of the altar is brought about [*conficio*] by the power of the words of Christ" (LtOrd 37). In one section of this letter, Francis gives a powerful admonition to his clerical brothers (meaning those ordained to any clerical rank—but in this case especially priests), which we can take as one of his quintessential statements on the Eucharist itself. Francis begins by chiding his clerical brothers to recognize their nearness to Christ:

> Listen my brothers: if the Blessed Virgin is so honored, as is becoming, because she carried Him in her most holy womb; if the Baptist trembled and did not dare to touch the holy head of God; if the tomb in which He lay for some time is held in veneration, how holy, just and fitting must be he who touches with his hands, receives in his heart and mouth, and offers to others to be received the One who is not now about to die but who will be victorious forever [*in eternum victurum*] and has been

glorified [*glorificatum*], *upon Whom the angels longed to gaze.* (1 Pet 1:12; LtOrd 21–22)

As we saw in the *Testament*, physical things and spaces aid Francis's memory and his articulation of the faith. Likewise, he turns his memory in this letter to bodies and sacred spaces, which he uses to remind the order's priests of their remarkable nearness to Christ, which belongs to all who hold and consume the body and blood of the Lord. Francis also focuses on how priests and all of us receive Jesus in the sacrament: into our hearts and mouths. By emphasizing heart and mouth, Francis picks out a simple truth: physical reception and eating of the sacrament allow the sacrament to do its spiritual work (though of course God can give us the grace of the sacrament however God wishes). The physical is the essential gateway to the spiritual for Francis. So attentive to bodies, Francis also highlights the qualities Jesus's body has in the Eucharist. He recognizes that while we honor Mary, John the Baptist, and Jesus's tomb for their nearness to a body that would or had suffered, the priest holds a body that cannot suffer, that is to be victorious and is already glorified. We receive and consume with our mouths the transformed body of the one who is transforming us.

This body that feeds the people of God, the priest holds and offers each day to the Father. Francis continues, "See your dignity...and be holy because He is holy....(Indeed) it is a great misery and a miserable weakness that when you have Him present in this way, you are concerned with anything else in the whole world" (LtOrd 23–25). Francis here lays down one of the most challenging aspects of Christian life: to focus on exactly what is before our faces. We are distracted by so many things, especially our past and our projection of the future and what it holds. Francis reminds us how much joy, how much less anxiety there is for us, when we focus upon the present moment and the person or thing that needs or deserves attention at just that moment. This is what it means to be simple. Simplicity is not about pretending to be stupid, or making cute mistakes, or being dull. Simplicity is about imitating God, who beholds all things and is present to all things with his undivided, undistracted gaze. Francis admonishes us to behold the body and blood of the Lord in the same way, training our mind upon the *one thing necessary* (see Luke 10:42). The Eucharist demands our focus and shows us how to focus on all the goods of our life.

Having chided priests—and all of us—about their nearness to Christ and having reminded them to pay attention to Christ's presence, Francis now dwells on the enormity of Christ's presence and the mystery that is being worked out in all of us:

> Let everyone be struck with fear, let the whole world tremble, and let the heavens exult when Christ the Son of the living God, is present on the altar in the hands of a priest! O wonderful loftiness and stupendous dignity! O sublime humility! O humble sublimity! The Lord of the universe, God and the Son of God, so humbles himself that for our salvation he hides himself under an ordinary piece of bread! Brothers, look at the humility of God, and *pour out your hearts before Him!* Humble yourselves that you may be exalted by Him! Hold back nothing of yourselves for yourselves that he who gives himself totally to you may receive you totally! (LtOrd 26–29)

Francis waits before the Eucharist like Elijah before his cave. The Lord is coming to us, but he is not in a whirlwind, or an earthquake, or a fiery conflagration. What brings Elijah to tremble in fear, to hide his face in his cloak, is a tiny whisper on the mountainside (1 Kgs 19:12). So, too, in the Eucharist. We do not typically see a grand transmogrification of bread and wine into the glorious body of Christ, still bearing the wounds that healed us. We do not hear angelic choirs praising the God of creation and redemption. Only the familiar signs of bread and wine meet us, which we believe in faith to be the Lord's own body and blood, living and true. God comes to us humbly, and Francis quakes before this humility. Zealous for us to embrace the humble Lord of Hosts, Francis pleads with us in a concluding flourish, which deserves repetition: "Look at the humility of God and pour out your hearts before Him! Hold back nothing of yourselves for yourselves that he who gives himself totally to you may receive you totally!" We are not approaching the passive presence of Christ but the consuming presence of the God who desires our transformation and wishes to bring it about through our reception of him. Christ holds none of himself back from us in this moment. He unites all that is God with all that is human and offers that whole to us. There is nothing else that we could receive or wish to receive. Francis enjoins us to imitate Christ with simplicity and humility and keep nothing for ourselves in that moment of reception but to offer ourselves completely to God. Giving God the totality of ourselves, God receives us totally, so that our own act of eating the body of Christ is itself an incorporation into Christ's body. This is why we must be prepared to receive the body of Christ through our conformity to the mind and life of Christ. For here at the altar, we are not just consuming but being consumed. We not only offer sacrifice; we are offered. The less that we put in the way of God receiving us, the more God can consume and incorporate us into the body of God's only Son.

The mystery of the Eucharist meets us in such simplicity: a man offering us food. Francis matches the mystery with his own simplicity, focusing simply on Christ and his transforming presence, a presence enabled by the Letter through which the Spirit works. This is the mystery of faith. With good reason then, in a passage from his "Admonitions," Francis reflects on the Eucharist and its relationship to the faith we have in God. Francis's "Admonitions" are a series of twenty-eight, typically brief texts. Scholars do not agree on the exact genesis of the text, nor on its precise contents. We may safely hold, however, that "The Admonitions" go back to words Francis said, preached, or dictated to be preserved. We may also safely hold that Admonition 1, the text that concerns us now, was part of the collection of texts and its first member. Francis therefore began his text of "Admonitions"—counsels for a Gospel life—with an admonition on the body and blood of the Lord.

The first Admonition begins as many of them do: with a string of biblical citations. The first passages are from John 14:6–9, which are related to Philip's request to see the Father. Jesus reminds Philip that to see him is to see the Father. Francis then picks up the thread:

> The Father dwells in *inaccessible light* (1 Tim 6:16), and *God is spirit* (John 4:24), and *no one has ever seen God* (John 1:18). Therefore. He cannot be seen except in the Spirit because *it is the Spirit that gives life; the flesh has nothing to offer* (John 6:63). But because He is equal to the Father, the Son is not seen by anyone other than the Father or other than the Holy Spirit. (Adm 1.4–7)

Francis again expresses one of the main problems of Christian life: we were made to see God but do not. Anselm of Canterbury (d. 1109) reflected on the same problem, occasioned by the same verse from 1 Timothy, in his famous *Proslogion.*

Anselm resolved this difficulty through the interior search for a bare thread of God's truth: the truth that God exists. Much as Francis's own search, Anselm understood that God must lead the search for God. But rather than trace out a truth about God, Francis takes another route. He acknowledges that God can only be seen by God. While the divine persons have clear sight of one another, our eyes see only the darkness of inaccessible light. If we wish to see under the brilliant shadow of God's wings, our eyes must accept the sight the Spirit gives; our own vision is too weak. As Francis continues, he arranges an illuminating parallel between apostolic faith in Jesus seen in the flesh and our faith in Jesus seen in the sacrament of the altar:

> All those who saw the Lord Jesus according to the humanity, therefore, and did not see and believe according to the Spirit and the Divinity that He is the true Son of God were condemned. Now in the same way, all those who see the sacrament sanctified by the words of the Lord upon the altar at the hands of the priest in the form of bread and wine and do not see and believe according to the Spirit and the Divinity that it is truly the Body and Blood of our Lord Jesus Christ, are condemned. (Adm 1.8–9)

Our eyes might immediately notice the word "condemned" because we do not expect to find it on Francis's lips, so peaceful do we understand him to be. Francis, however, often speaks this bluntly about the faith. He clearly believed in the necessity and efficacy of the sacraments. Even here, though, we should tread lightly. Dante's *Divine Comedy*, a magnificent medieval expression of sin and salvation, gives no simplistic portrait of condemnation, and we might think the same is ultimately true for Francis.

This passage also highlights that the visible is the gateway to the invisible. But here Francis explains that our assent to the invisible reality cloaked before us is enabled by that same invisible reality. The Spirit causes our sight to grow wide and sharp enough to climb the heights and depths of faith; we cannot do this of our own accord. There was no magic look about Jesus that caused Simon and Andrew, James and John, to drop their nets. Divinity does not glow. *God is Spirit*, Francis reminds us, and *no one has ever seen God*. What the apostles saw and confessed about Jesus, they saw and confessed by the Spirit. So, too, we who confess the mystery of faith upon the altar, confess it by the Spirit's power, not our own. Our faith must be humble.

Francis continues his admonition, shifting from seeing and confessing to eating and incorporation.

> *This is my Body and the Blood of my new covenant* (Mark 14:22, 24); and *Whoever eats my flesh and drinks my blood has eternal life* (John 6:55). It is the Spirit of the Lord therefore, that lives in its faithful that receives the Body and Blood of the Lord. All others who do not share in this same Spirit and presume to receive him eat and drink *judgment on themselves*. (1 Cor 11:29; Adm 1.10–12)

The Spirit enables us to see and confess. The Spirit also receives in us and enables us to be transformed. If we combine this passage with the stirring conclusion of the previous passage from the "Letter to the Entire Order," Francis's understanding of eucharistic reception becomes clearer. To be received by Christ in the Eucharist, we must offer ourselves to him totally. Only the Spirit can enable us to do this.

Like Christ, we can empty ourselves, grasping at nothing, and offer ourselves in total humility to God and to humanity. Our reception of Christ requires that we look upon a man offering us simple food and see by the Spirit's power the Lord who restores all things. When we consume the mystery, the Spirit consumes it within us, who dwells in us, and enables us to see and believe and do.

Francis's words now change to an impassioned plea:

> Therefore *children how long will you be hard of heart?* (Ps 4:3). Why do you not know the truth and believe in the Son of God (John 9:35)? Behold each day he humbles himself as when he came *from the royal throne* (Wis 18:15) into the Virgin's womb; each day he himself comes to us, appearing humbly; each day he comes down *from the bosom of the Father* (John 1:18) upon the altar in the hands of a priest. (Adm 1.14–18)

Francis's mind again turns to spaces and places dwelt in by God and the action of God who keeps coming to us humbly. Francis trembles at the thought. Our pride must not hold us back. Here we must meet God just as God meets us: with humility. We do so with and by the Spirit.

Francis concludes this admonition by revisiting the parallel between the apostles' faith in Christ and our own:

> And as they saw only his flesh by an insight of their flesh, yet believed that he was God as they contemplated him with their spiritual eyes, let us, as we see bread and wine with our bodily eyes, see and firmly believe that they are his most holy Body and Blood living and true. And in this way the Lord is always with his faithful, as he himself

says: *Behold I am with you until the end of the age.* (Matt 28:20; Adm 1.20–22)

Our physical eyes need the Spirit's presence to behold the Lord, who cannot be seen by our own power, though he is living and true. The Eucharist is a feast that tempers us, instructs us, and transforms us. At the altar, we can allow the Spirit to animate our faith and to help us put "every thought captive to obey Christ" (2 Cor 10:5). When we accept the Spirit's aid, we can see the Letter more clearly and can cleave to the presence of him who is present to us.

The humility modeled and learned in the Eucharist hopefully flows into the way we live our daily lives, impacting how we act toward family, neighbor, and stranger. Surely, when we exercise humility toward others, our humility toward God also grows; and so, our interior formation and external action mutually reinforce one another. Exercising humility, eucharistic humility, is especially important for those of us accorded any authority or power. Francis states this clearly in his brief "Letter to the Rulers of the Peoples," which we may take as our third text of meditation. What animated Francis to compose this letter and when he did so is not known. Whatever the inspiration, Francis's letter reflects ancient and medieval notions of justice, and justice is something the poor always hope their rulers possess.

Francis begins his letter to these authorities with deference and a wish for peace but quickly turns to his purpose:

Reflect and see that the day of death draws very close [*appropinquat*]. With all possible respect, therefore, I beg you not to forget the Lord because of this world's cares and preoccupations and not to turn away from his commandments, for all those who leave him in oblivion and turn away from his commandments are cursed and will be left in oblivion by him. (LtR 2–3)

What we store in our memory is often the impetus for our action. Francis forces three memories upon the rulers of the peoples: their own death, the Lord, and his commandments. In fact, this passage is more about memory and forgetfulness than the English can capture. In Latin "oblivion" is tied not just to destruction (as our English ears may assume) but specifically to forgetfulness. We may therefore translate those words in the passage differently as "all those who forget [the Lord]...will be forgotten by [the Lord]." To forget the Lord, the one memory we must hold onto, is fittingly punished by his forgetting us before the Father. Insistent that rulers must remember the Lord, Francis is equally insistent that they must remember the commandments. Here we cannot forget that the Decalogue begins with the command to worship the one God and proceeds from that point toward the just treatment of others. In other words, if justice is granting to each person what he or she deserves (an ancient definition assumed in medieval culture), then justice rightly begins by extending justice to the source of Justice. "Let us give thanks to the Lord our God," the priest prompts us in the liturgy; and we respond, "It is right and just." The liturgy allows us to give justice to God, and from that place true justice, God's justice, may be extended. The liturgy further reminds us that we can give none of that justice on our own, but only with the Lord's own words and the Spirit's power. So, Francis next reminds the rulers that all the power they seem to have will vanish, and that the greater the power they had in this world, the greater shall be their punishment in the next, should they use their power poorly (LtR 4–5). If the rulers forget their own death is nigh and assume their power is their own, then they will be exposed to judgement.

How shall these rulers learn what is necessary to be spared and be sparing? Francis turns them to the Eucharist: "Therefore I strongly advise you, my Lords, to put aside all care and preoccupation, do true penance, and receive the most holy Body and Blood of our Lord Jesus Christ kindly [*benigne*] in holy remembrance of him (LtR 6)." Francis admonishes the rulers clearly: receive the sacrament of memory, where God's humility can teach you humility, where God's justice can show you justice, where Christ lays himself down and feeds his people. To make his point further, Francis tells these rulers to receive Christ in the sacrament "kindly" (a word he uses often), which we must imagine is just the way he hopes they will receive and act toward their own people. But something else stirs in Francis's choice of words—*benigne*—something he may not have fully realized himself.

Scattered throughout the many genres of medieval theology and medieval devotional life is a particular series of attributes that theologians and other writers thought (following ancient precedents) were appropriately but not exclusively applied to individual persons of the Trinity. They called these attributes *appropriations*. To the Father was accorded power, to the Son wisdom, and to the Holy Spirit benevolence (*benevolentia*) or kindness (*benignitas*). It was this *benignitas* that God extended in creating all things. When the Spirit hovered over the waters of creation, it hovered out of the depth of God's kindness to bring forth, for no other reason than love itself, a world of vibrant life where that love could be shared. Christ extended this same *benignitas* in his incarnation and death, a path he also took out of love for us. To receive Christ in the sacrament *benigne*, then, is to receive him by the Spirit, as we saw Francis emphasize in "The Admonitions." To receive him so, we might further say, is to return that *benignitas* to the Father through Christ out of our love for his mercy in creating and recreating us.

Francis thus admonishes these rulers, indeed all of us, to receive the Lord's own body and blood as incorporation into the life of the triune God and to let that life illuminate our minds and actions. Francis further instructs these rulers to make an announcement every evening, by a messenger or some sign, "that praise and thanksgiving may be given by all the people to the all powerful Lord God" (LtR 7). Francis's words are clear but subtle. He explicitly names God as "all powerful Lord God," thereby indicating that the lordship of these rulers, whose power and lordship is derivative, is an office and a gift. To care for this gift well, they must be just and call their people to praise God. In closing, Francis, like a prophet, offers the rulers the choice of curse or blessing: "If you do not do this, know that, on the day of judgment you must render an account before the Lord Your God, Jesus Christ. Let those who keep this writing with them and observe it know that they will be blessed by the Lord God" (LtR 8–9).

Francis's simple attention to the Letter of the Eucharist, across the texts chosen here, displays the humility of the all-powerful Lord God. Francis begs us to make this humility our own, to look upon the mystery of faith with humility, to receive Christ in just the way he comes to us, and to allow Christ through the Spirit to bring into our bodies and souls the transformation he wishes to occur. This humility, this attention to the Letter through which the Spirit stirs and acts, is also a hallmark of Francis's life of prayer, to which we now turn.

3

Prayer/*Gratiarum actio*

Once, as Francis traveled, the rain did not stop (*AC* 120). This must have happened more than once, but this particular instance stuck in someone's memory. Francis rode a horse that dreary day, a liberty the Rule of the brothers allowed to those who were sick and weak. As the rain poured down, the time for the next *hora*, or period, of prayer arrived. Francis dismounted and stood along the road, so that he could say his Office properly. "*Deus in adiutorium meum intende*—God come to my assistance," he began. Water filled the earth and air around him and he filled his mouth with the psalmist's praise. As the day and the rain rolled by, Francis kept pausing along the way to say his hours, kept getting off his horse and standing in the rain. *Deus in adiutorium meum intende*. Maybe he smirked a little, let the rain play on his hands and face; maybe he didn't care about the wet and the mud. Sister Water, as Francis's "Canticle of Creatures" sings, is "humble and precious and chaste" (*CtC* 7): she can't get in the way of this sacred task, to say the words of the Lord. Francis closed the *hora* with the blessing and was up on his horse again. He said, either at the time or in reference to the moment, "If the body wants to eat its food in peace and quiet, and both it and the body eventually will become food for worms, in what peace and quiet should the soul receive its food, which is God Himself!" (AC 120).

Of all the forms of prayer that Francis employed, he cultivated and clung to the saying of the Office—the cycle of Psalms that marks the day and surrounds the eucharistic celebration. The tradition of praying the Psalms throughout the day goes back to the Jewish people. The apostles, guided by the Spirit of the Lord, continued a practice they already knew, and the psalms became part of the Church's prayer. As the Christian centuries wore on, praying the Psalms became praying the Office or Liturgy of the Hours, which grew to include other scriptural readings, readings from saints, songs, prayers, and modifications for feasts and seasons. The Office has often been understood as a practical way to fulfill Paul's joyful admonition: "Pray without ceasing" (1 Thes 5:17). In the Rule without a Papal Seal (or Earlier Rule), a document that articulates the life of the young order and its structures, Francis and his brothers enjoined the saying of the Office in the following way:

> The Lord says: *This kind of devil cannot come out except through fasting and prayer* (Mark 9:28); and again: *When you fast do not become gloomy like the hypocrites* (Matt 6:16). For this reason let all the brothers, whether clerical or lay, recite the Divine Office, the praises and prayers, as is required of them. (ER III.1–3)

Perhaps when we hear Mark 9:28 used to recommend the Office, we imagine that the fasting and prayer the Lord demands is something only meant for that moment, to cast out an imminent threat. Francis and his brothers imagined something different. Effective fasting and prayer is a constant discipline, aided by the rhythm the Office establishes. Dedication to the Letter allows the Spirit to work as it wills and conquer the forces that accuse and assail us. Francis therefore orders that the Office be said by the brothers in many of his texts and indicates in his *Testament* that he desires to keep saying the Office despite his growing weaknesses (*Test* 29). He also reserves harsh punishment in the *Testament* for those brothers who refuse to say the Office (*Test* 30–33).

As we might expect, saying the Office was not enough. Francis, as we have seen, always wanted more. In addition to the Office, Francis said the "Little Office of the Blessed Virgin," a series of psalms and prayers that honored the Mother of God, which had become popular by his time. Even this, however, was not enough. Not long after his embrace of religious life, around 1205, Francis began constructing psalms and prayers into what became his own Office, so great was his craving for the Letter. Francis chose a theme for his Office—the passion of Jesus. We should pause over this act and allow it to form a central part of how we view Francis: he composed his own Office! We might view Francis's Office as a stretching out of the prayer he recalls saying in churches in the *Testament* (*Test* 5). Since this Office contains prayers written by Francis and its structure was his own design, it provides us with an intimate view of Francis's prayer life, of the words and images he wanted to impress upon his memory. Sadly, perhaps only Clare of Assisi ever bothered to pray this Office as Francis did. In any case, few people prayed it, despite its beauty and power, and today we ascribe to Francis a prayer he never wrote or said (the so-called Peace Prayer). Examining this Office can bring us closer to Francis and the Lord he followed.[1]

---

1. Anyone wishing to say this Office can find it available in formats that aid its daily recitation. *Office of the Passion of Francis of Assisi* is available from Tau Publishing. The same format is also available from the Franciscan Institute.

Francis's Office of the Passion, as the rubrics of the text tell us, had a clear structure. Each hour began with an Our Father, followed by the Glory Be, a constant refrain of liturgical praise in any Office. Next came a series of praises called the "Praises to Be Said at All the Hours." After these praises, Francis said a collect, or prayer. Next, he pronounced an antiphon that preceded and followed a psalm for that hour. The Office closed with a concluding blessing (OfP). Although this may sound like it has many parts, Francis's Office was not long. We can look at each element of this Office to obtain a better sense for this original prayer that Francis said daily.

Looking closely at the exact phrasing of the Our Father in the rubric, it appears that Francis has expanded the Our Father, adding "O most Holy" to the familiar prayer: "O our Most Holy Father—*Sanctissime Pater noster.*" Notably, Francis also wrote a text on the Our Father that begins in just this way. The text is often called a commentary or exposition of the Our Father, but it is more like an extended meditation on the Our Father, a way for Francis to lengthen the prayer's Letter with the Spirit's aid. Francis possibly said this extended Our Father as part of his Office. In any case, the extended text shows us how Francis may have thought about the Our Father whenever he prayed it. Given the text's length, we will only meditate on a few moments of this extended prayer, especially those connected to Francis's eucharistic devotion.

Francis begins his meditative Our Father with extensive praise of the Father himself: "O *our Father* most holy: our creator, redeemer, consoler, and savior" (PrOF 1). In this opening address, Francis intuits that the Trinity works together, and so the Father can be called by titles we might more naturally accord to the Son or the Spirit. As Francis continues, he builds into one of his most characteristic ways of praising God in all his prayers: praising God's supreme goodness. His meditation continues: "*Who art in heaven*: in the angels and the saints, enlightening them to know, for you Lord are light; inflaming them to love, for you Lord are love; dwelling in them and filling them with blessedness [*beatitudinem*] for you Lord are the supreme good, the eternal good, from whom all good comes, without whom there is no good" (PrOF 2). *Good* and the *Supreme Good* are the words Francis uses most consistently in his praises of God throughout all his writings. Francis's desire to praise God in prayer, to give thanks that God is good and the giver of all good is a "eucharistic" mode of praying, for *eucharist* means "thanksgiving." Another eucharistic connection emerges in Francis's praises here. All the good that Francis understands the saints and angels to have, they have in the same way Francis understands us to believe in and receive the body and blood of Christ—through God's own power and indwelling presence. Receiving the Eucharist then, in the way Francis conceives of it, is a foretaste of heavenly life, where God receives and fills us with the good that God is. Later in his meditative extension of the Our Father, Francis explicitly connects his thoughts to the Eucharist. Meditating on the phrase *Give us this day our daily bread*, Francis prays "give us today your beloved Son, our Lord Jesus Christ in remembrance, understanding and reverence of that love which he had for us and of those things that He said and did and suffered for us" (PrOF 6). *Our daily bread* is something that transcends earthly food for Francis; it is Jesus and the memory of him, a memory that can sustain and guide our thoughts and actions.

We can further see how the memory of Jesus, at the center of Francis's extended praises, guides two other parts of his Our Father. When Francis prays *Your will be done on earth as it is in heaven*, he offers his longest extension, utilizing Deuteronomy 6:5 as restated in Luke 10:27, the great commandment: *You shall love the Lord your God with all your heart, with all your being, with all your strength, and with all your mind and your neighbor as yourself*. Francis prays that he may focus all his powers on God's love and then hopes that its unifying power may spill out to everyone whom he encounters. He says, "And let us love our neighbors as ourselves by drawing them all to Your love with our whole strength, by rejoicing in the good of others just as in our own, by suffering with others in the evils that befall them, and *by giving offense to no one*" (PrOF 5; see 2 Cor 6:3). Love is how the Father's will is done. This love, a love that endures all things (1 Cor 13:7), will be no easy task; we will need to be sustained on the daily bread of memory— the Lord himself. God's love, revealed in the beloved Son, is also what enables us to forgive fully. Thus, Francis prays, "*Forgive us our debts* [*debita*]: through your ineffable mercy, through the power of the passion of your beloved Son....*As we forgive those indebted to us*: And what we do not fully forgive, make us Lord forgive completely" (PrOF 7–8). When Francis spoke of eucharistic reception, he challenged us to offer everything to God in that moment, to keep nothing back from God in our reception of the daily bread of memory that sustains us. In the Eucharist, we must try to offer our whole self to God. Francis knows this total surrender to God is difficult. Here, in his meditation on the Our Father, he recognizes that it is also difficult to totally forgive those who have wronged us. But by offering ourselves and forgiveness completely, even to enemies, we follow the Lord in his passion and display in ourselves something of the mystery we consume upon the altar. Only God can enable us to do this.

Francis's meditation continues through the end of the Our Father and then offers a Glory Be. The offering of a Glory Be further suggests that Francis's meditative Our Father may have been a part of his Office, since this doxology concludes other parts of Francis's Office and the other Offices he prayed, but we cannot know for certain.

After the Our Father, the next part of Francis's Office is the "Praises to Be Said at All the Hours," an original composition of Francis. These "Praises" have a clear structure. Each strophe contains a blessing or word of praise, followed by the refrain: "And let us praise and exalt him above all forever" (*GOfP* 41; PrH 1). That refrain is adapted from the song of the three men in the furnace in the Book of Daniel (Dan 3:52–90). Francis's other model for his hymn of praise stems from scenes in the Book of Revelation, especially those pertaining to the Lamb in Revelation 4. As Laurent Gallant and André Cirino note in *The Geste of the Great King: Office of the Passion of Francis of Assisi* (*GOfP*), Francis punctuates each hour of his Office of the Passion by praising the Lord's victory as the lamb who was slain. Gallant and Cirino further observe that with these "Praises," drawn from the heavenly liturgy of Revelation 4, Francis builds a "spiritual cathedral" in his mind "in which resounds an unending symphony of celestial praise" (*GOfP* 213). In this way, no matter where Francis was when he prayed his Office, he entered into the worship of heaven and gave praise to "one who is not now about to die but who will be victorious forever and is glorified [*glorificatum*], *upon Whom the angels longed to gaze*" (1 Pet 1:12; LtOrd 22). We will look at these praises a little more closely.

The praises that Francis said seven times a day begin, "Holy, Holy, Holy, Lord God Almighty, Who is and Who was and Who is to come (cf. Rev 4:8). And let us praise and glorify him forever" (Dan 3:57; PrH 1). With these words, Francis effectively becomes one of the fantastic creatures who praises God in the Book of Revelation and invites us to do the same. As the "Praises" continue, God and the Lamb are praised (2–3); the whole Trinity is praised (4); creation is called upon to praise God (5–8); and finally, the two halves of the Glory Be are used as the last two strophes (9–10).

Francis's creativity in this song of praise lies not in the words but in their arrangement, for nearly every word is from the Scriptures or an existing liturgy. Francis's style here is akin to what he finds in the eucharistic liturgy: we offer the Lord his own Letters and allow the Spirit to work. These "Praises," furthermore, are simply that: praises. Francis asks for nothing in them. In this regard, they are a prayer of total humility, words drawn from God's own words, gifted to us in the Scriptures, to do nothing but praise God and invite all of creation (seen and unseen) to that praise. This is humble, eucharistic praise of God.

As a good student of the liturgy, Francis next gathers the praises of his fervent scriptural hymn into an original collect, a prayer (PrH 11). The prayer is simple and pure. I have arranged it vertically on the page to slow us down:

> All powerful,
> most holy,
> most high,
> supreme God:
> all good,
> supreme good,
> totally good,
> you who alone are good;
> may we give back to you [*tibi reddamus*]
> all praise,
> all glory,
> all thanks,
> all honor,
> all blessing,
> and all good.
> So be it.
> So be it.
> Amen.

We could dwell on each of Francis's words and extend this prayer just as he extended the Our Father. I will offer only a few observations. Francis said this prayer seven times a day as part of his Office. Earlier in his extension of the Our Father, Francis praised God's goodness in the same way, and in other texts Francis offers similar praise (2LtF 61–62; ER 17, 17–19; 23, 9). God's goodness and the necessity for us to give that good back is one of the clearest themes in Francis's life and writings. Perhaps we might presume, however, that in an Office dedicated to Christ's passion, Francis should praise the cross directly, or some other aspect of Christ's suffering. Instead, Francis's simplicity takes in the cross, takes in creation, and arrives in prayer at God who is good, who creates all things, who restores all things, and who will come to put all things aright. By this prayer, at each hour of the day, Francis remembers God's goodness in creation and redemption and remembers his own response of praise. The prayer further reminds him that no good belongs to him and no good is his to keep, for only God is good. For this reason, Francis must return all good to God in praise. That "return," voiced as *tibi reddamus*, "may we give back to you," or "let us give back to you" is the prayer's only petition; it is Francis's genuine need—the will to offer himself totally to God's praise and to be formed by the praise he gives.

Having gathered his praises into a simple prayer, Francis now prays an original antiphon that precedes and follows the psalm text of his Office at every hour. In this antiphon he turns to the Mother of God:

> Holy Virgin Mary, among women born into the world, there is no one like you. Daughter and servant of the most high and supreme King, the heavenly Father, Mother of our most holy Lord Jesus Christ, Spouse of the Holy Spirit, pray for

us with Saint Michael the Archangel, all the powers of heaven, and all the saints, before [apud] your
most holy beloved Son, Lord and teacher. (OfP
antiphon, *FA:ED* 1:141)

Once again, we must recall that Francis prayed this little
text seven, or perhaps fourteen times a day (if he said it to
begin and conclude the psalm of the hour). These are words
he brought to mind about Mary all throughout the day, in the
context of his little Office. The antiphon borrows from other
Marian prayers and crystallizes much of the way the Church
typically invokes Mary. The antiphon is also typical of Francis
and his Italian upbringing, in that it also invokes St. Michael,
whose appearance in Gargano, Italy, in the early Middle Ages
made St. Michael into something of an Italian saint. Francis uses familiar titles for Mary (daughter, servant, mother,
spouse), which then relate her to the trinitarian persons. The
hinge of the antiphon is "pray for us," although Francis does
not specify his need. We might guess that his need is help
fulfilling what he had just asked for in his prayer, to return
all good to God. Francis does specify who Mary leads in
prayer—the whole celestial court—and he specifies to whom
their prayer is addressed—Mary's Son, Lord, and Teacher.

Gallant and Cirino (*GofP* 222) have pointed out that
when Francis calls Jesus "Lord and Teacher [*Dominum et Mag-
istrum*]," he recalls John 13:12–15 as it is in the Latin Vulgate:
"You call me Teacher and Lord [*Magister et Domine*], and rightly
so, for indeed I am. If I, therefore, the Lord and Teacher
[*Dominus et Magister*], have washed your feet, you ought to
wash one another's feet. I have given you an example so that
as I have done for you, you should also do." This passage is
a motif found throughout Francis's writings, and he wishes
to hear the passage in the closing hours of his life (as we
shall see). Since the passage relates to the Last Supper, we

are right to see it in connection with the Eucharist. We are also right to imagine that Francis would have interpreted the Synoptics (who mention the institution of the Eucharist but not the foot washing) and John (who recounts the foot washing but no institution) as working together in their portrayal of the Last Supper. The humility Francis sees in the way Jesus comes to us in the Eucharist is therefore tied to Jesus's other major gesture at the Last Supper, foot washing. Jesus, the great teacher, shows us how to pray and live at the Last Supper, something we can see him do at every Eucharist through the sight the Spirit gives. The Lord and Master is a teacher of humility, a humility that marks Francis's life of prayer, since he desires nothing for himself but to give God fitting praise through the words that God has already given. Francis's Marian antiphon places his psalms between the arms of the same mother who gave birth to Jesus and witnessed his death. Francis will praise Mary elsewhere as "the virgin made Church" (SalBVM 1). To place his psalms between Mary's arms is therefore to place his psalms in the Church, to pray them with the Church, in the bosom of faith.

After the antiphon, Francis prayed a psalm. The sequence of psalms Francis prayed throughout the day in his Office moved him through the moments of Jesus's passion: his prayer in the garden of Gethsemane, his arrest, trial, agony, death, and resurrection. Francis composed fifteen psalms in all. Half of his psalms were for the bulk of the year and the others for particular seasons. Most of the psalms that make up Francis's Office are original constructions made from different scriptural verses, different Letters of Scripture, that he brought together with the Spirit's help to remember a specific event. In a few cases, Francis simply used an existing biblical psalm without any modification. Each of Francis's psalms, in the context of his Office, deserves prayerful reading. Here, we will only focus on parts of psalms six and seven.

Francis used the sixth of his psalms for the hour of None, the ninth hour, or about three in the afternoon, the time of Christ's death. As we might expect, Francis employs many words from Psalm 22, the psalm on Jesus's own lips as he gives up his life to the Father (Mark 15:34). Accordingly, the first half of Francis's psalm is distressing, describing Christ's suffering, but, like Psalm 22, Francis's sixth psalm composition turns sharply, moving from suffering to victory and joy. The hinge of Francis's psalm is verse 11, *"I have slept and I have risen* (Ps 3:6) and my most holy Father *has received me with glory* (Ps 72:24)."* Suddenly, the pain and suffering of Christ give way to his glory, his victory. Verse 15 describes this victory further: *"Blessed be the Lord, the God of Israel* (Luke 1:68), *who has redeemed the souls of his servants* (Ps 34:23) with his own most holy blood *and who will not abandon all who hope in him* (Ps 34:23)."* Francis's psalm composition recalls the throne room of the "Praises to Be Said at All the Hours," where praise is given to the Lamb who was slain. The psalm also points to the liturgy, where the Lord's blood is given to us as a saving cup.

The final verse of Francis's psalm 6 draws us even further out in time, further out to the ends of Christ's victory, into a final prayerful admonition: "And we know that he is coming, that he will come to judge justice" (cf. Ps 95:13). There is no greater warning about our own lack of justice than to recall Christ's coming judgment in the context of the injustice done to him. Yet this injustice was not the end, for God turned this injustice into absolute victory over death and sin. For our justice to reflect God's justice, the cross must anoint it. As we look upon the whole of this psalm, we see that Francis does not use the psalm or the hour of the day to celebrate gore and suffering. Rather, he follows the Scriptures and the faith of the Church, moving from Christ's suffering to his victory, to his coming in judgement. Francis reminded himself daily of this complex of themes at the hour of Christ's death.

Francis utilized his seventh psalm composition for Vespers, prayer as daylight fades. In contrast to his sixth psalm, psalm 7 is a rousing celebration of the story of salvation and God's kingship. *"All you nations clap your hands, shout to God with a voice of gladness"* (Ps 47:2), psalm 7 begins. The praise continues: "For the Most Holy Father of heaven, *our King before all ages* (Ps 74:12), sent his beloved Son from on high, and *has brought salvation in the midst of the earth* (Ps 72:12)." Having invoked the incarnation, Francis next calls all things to the praise of God— the heavens and earth, the sea and the fields (OfP Ps 7, 4). This call to praise continues for a few verses but like his sixth psalm composition, psalm 7 suddenly changes direction. Here the psalm doubles back to the passion: *"Take up your bodies and carry his holy cross* (cf. Luke 14:27) and *follow his most holy commands even to the end* (cf. 1 Pet 2:21). Let the whole earth tremble before his face, tell among the nations that the Lord has ruled from a tree* (Ps 96:9–10)" (OfP Ps 7, 8–9). Francis offers us in prayer the complex mystery of responding to the unity of the cross and resurrection: Christ has risen in glory from an awful death and calls us to the same glory through the carrying of his cross.

From Good Friday to the Feast of the Ascension, Francis's seventh psalm ended with the Lord ruling from a tree. Francis, taught by the Church's prayer, realized that certain times and seasons called for different words. Thus, from the Feast of the Ascension until Advent, Francis added the following verses to his seventh psalm: "He ascended into heaven and is seated at the right hand of the most holy Father in heaven. *O God be exalted above the heavens and above all the earth be your glory* (Ps 57:12). We know that he is coming, that he will come to judge justice (Ps 95:13)" (OfP Ps 7, 10–11). The additional verses begin with a line from the Nicene Creed, which Francis has fitted to sing God's praise. The last verse repeats the final verse of Francis's sixth psalm and reminds us again of Christ coming in judgment. When we reflect on the verses that precede these, we know that Christ's judgment is again linked to the cross, and not just his cross, but our willingness to take up his cross. The context of both psalm compositions, however, tells us that this admonition about judgment is also joyful: it is the Lord who is coming! He will judge us justly. How different from the judgment of those we constantly fear in this world, whose judgment often has no part in the good that is God. There can be no injustice with God. He will not judge us in secret. He will not praise us in one place and slander us in another; he will not gather a ring of enemies about us in the dark, conspiring with anyone who will listen to ensure our condemnation. He lived that horror. The lord of justice will judge us in the open, with true justice.

After the saying of the psalm, Francis said the Glory Be and then may have repeated his Marian antiphon. Francis then concluded each hour of his Office with a simple blessing: "Let us bless the Lord God living and true! Let us always give back [*referamus*] to him praise, glory, honor, blessing and all good. Amen. Amen. So be it. So be it" (*FA:ED* 1:141). The final blessing reflects the prayer Francis said earlier in the Office and sends him forth with a simple truth ringing in his memory: giving all good back to God is a sacred task. Francis tried to fulfill this task daily at least by offering back to God the Letters of Scripture God gifted to us. Francis's concluding blessing also alludes to the primary way by which we give all good back to God: by offering him the body and blood of his Son, an offering made possible only by the Lord's Letter and Spirit. We can see this eucharistic connection if we notice that Francis's concluding blessing specifically invokes "the Lord God living and true." In the Admonitions, Francis uses these same words to refer to the Lord's most holy body and blood (Adm 1, 21), and in his "First Letter to the Custodians." Francis asserts that when the Lord's most holy body and blood are sacrificed, all should "praise, glorify, and honor on bended knee the Lord

God living and true" (1LtCus 7). Francis's concluding blessing therefore names the eucharistic Lord who is living and true, the body and blood around which the letters of every Office wheel, whose Spirit gives life and sense to the words spoken and to the lips of the speaker.

By praying three Offices daily—the Church's own, one dedicated to the Virgin Mary, and another he crafted to remember the Passion—Francis kept filling his mind and memory with the words, deeds, and praises of God. The fact that Francis prayed a triple Office suggests how important this mode of prayer was to him. The importance of the Office to Francis also emerges in other ways. One of the most famous churches in the story of Francis is the Portiuncula, also called St. Mary of the Angels. Today, the little church stands adorned and enshrined in a much larger Basilica, built long after Francis first encountered its humble stones. In Francis's time this old church outside Assisi's walls was owned by the Benedictines. One story tells that as the number of brothers around Francis grew, he realized that they needed a place to pray the Office properly (*AC* 56). So, Francis made a deal with the Benedictines to rent the Portiuncula in exchange for a yearly basket of fish. A church beloved by Francis, his brothers, and their devotees, was loved in the beginning as a poor place to give service to God through the Word.

Something else Francis did further shows us his devotion to the Office. While Francis prized praying in churches with the Letters gifted by the Spirit, he also prized praying in secluded caves, in the forest, in lonely places (Mark 1:35), and on the way (regardless of the weather), as the medieval lives of Francis recount. At some point, Francis realized that it would be good to offer guidelines for brothers who wished to stay at "official" lonely places—hermitages—like Le Celle, La Verna, and others previously mentioned. With the image of Martha and Mary in mind (Luke 10:38–42), Francis therefore composed a brief Rule for Hermitages. He stipulates that two of the brothers should act as mothers, and two should act as sons (RH 1–2). The mothers must keep people away from their sons so that they have time and space to pray (RH 7–8). When it seems right, the brothers can swap their roles (RH 10). Francis indicates that the one activity the mothers and sons enjoy together is praying the Office. In his only direct use of the Scriptures in this Rule, Francis characterizes their rising and praying the Office together as to *"seek first the kingdom of God and his justice"* (Matt 6:33; RH 3). While at a hermitage, then, the brothers soak in the justice of God through prayerful praise. Other forms of prayer were surely employed at these places of spiritual training and renewal, but the Office is to be the rhythm of their days.

Francis prayed not only the Office but also made exhortations, salutations, lists of praises, and brief formulaic prayers. Besides these recorded prayers, the medieval lives of Francis report the power of his prayer (both before and after his death), describe him praying with songs and tears and groans, tell of his meditative and contemplative practices and states, and stand in awe of the phenomena that sometimes occurred when he prayed. While any of these stories are worth our consideration, I prefer to conclude this chapter by taking us back to an earlier sequence in Francis's life, a time when Francis had perhaps never prayed the Letters of the Office, when all he seemed to have was his own sensitivity to the Spirit. The sequence recalls our meditation on Francis's *Testament*.

The *Legend of the Three Companions*, a text of remembrance written in the 1240s, relates that after Francis returned from a journey to Apulia seeking knightly glory, he feasted with friends and picked up the bill, as he often did (L3C 3.7). As they left the residence, they filled Assisi's dark streets with song. Francis, as the head of the group, was supposed to lead his friends in pretend triumph through the city with a scepter. Instead, Francis drifted to the back. Something strange was happening. He wasn't singing like his friends but was focused in thought (*diligenter meditando*):

And behold, he was suddenly visited by the Lord, and his heart was filled with such tenderness that he was unable to speak or move. He could only feel and hear this marvelous sweetness; it left him so estranged from any sensation that, as he himself said later, even if he had been completely cut to pieces, he would not have been able to move. (*L3C* 3.7)

What was he so focused on, his friends suddenly wondered, seeing him in such an odd state? They teased him that he was thinking of taking a wife, and Francis agreed, but he was thinking of Lady Poverty.

Something began to change in Francis that night walking home, a change made by the Spirit. Francis was receptive to the Spirit's movement, we learn, for shortly thereafter he began to think less and less of himself and the things he formerly loved. He sought out hidden places to pray and began to feel himself more and more responsive to the Spirit as the tenderness that visited him that night drove him into prayer, even in public places (*L3C* 3.8). Some citizens reacted to him with scorn and bewilderment. Francis pressed on, following the Spirit's lead. Already a man generous to the poor, Francis became more so, giving away money, giving away food, giving away the clothes on his back. He went to Rome, on business or pilgrimage or both, and poured out his money in the church of St. Peter and then swapped clothes with a poor man to beg alms in broken French. When he returned to Assisi, further changed, he still didn't know what to do with his life and kept turning to prayer to find an answer. One day, we are told, he thought he had an answer—to drop all his loves that were formed by the flesh (*carnaliter*), for they would only end in bitterness and could not bring him nearer to the sweetness and tenderness he had felt that night in Assisi's streets (*L3C* 4.1). Not long after this, Francis encountered a leper while out riding his horse. He dismounted, gave him a coin, and kissed him. He then moved to the *leprosaria* and "stayed among [the lepers] and served them with humility" (*L3C* 4.12).

But had he found an answer? What was he to do? He left the lepers for a time, continued praying, and continued searching. Not much time had passed when he was out walking and came near San Damiano, an old and crumbling church outside Assisi's walls, and "he was told in the Spirit to go inside for prayer" (*L3C* 5.13). Humble and obedient before the Spirit's prompting, "he began to pray intensely before an image of the Crucified" (*L3C* 5.13). Some manuscripts give the text of the prayer he said at this moment in his own Umbrian dialect. This is a translation:

> O most high
> and glorious God,
> enlighten the darkness of my heart
> and give me
> right faith,
> certain hope,
> and perfect charity,
> sense and knowledge,
> Lord,
> that I may carry out
> your holy and true command. (PrCr)

The Lord did not delay in answering Francis's sincere cry for transformation and direction. While Francis was praying from his heart in the half-light of San Damiano's musty shadows and ruined walls, the old cross, forgotten in this neglected holy place, spoke with devotion and kindness (*pie ac benigne*): "'Francis, don't you see that my house is being destroyed? Go, then, and repair [*repara*] it for me.' Stunned and trembling, Francis said: 'I will do so gladly Lord'" (*L3C* 5.13).

And he did.

Francis dedicated himself to prayer. His life of prayer grew. He followed the Spirit's lead in the streets of Assisi and was led to lepers and old crosses. He followed the Spirit into the depth of the Letters of the Office. His mind and memory wanted more, and he crafted his Office of the Passion. He clung to those words at all times of the day and in all kinds of weather. That dedication to the Letter in prayer, he matched with dedication to the Letter in his life, a life he did not live alone but with brothers and sisters who joined him on his Gospel path.

4

Life/*Sancta operatio*

Francis stepped out of tiny San Damiano and found the priest. He gave him a fistful of coins and said, "My Lord, I beg you, buy some oil and keep the light before the Crucified burning continually. When this money runs out, I will again give you as much as you need" (L3C 5.13). To keep a light burning in a church was a sign of piety, a sign of devotion, of prayers and intentions still smoldering and flickering in the shadows. The writers of the *Legend of the Three Companions* note that from this moment forward Francis's "heart was wounded and it melted when remembering the Lord's passion. While he lived he bore the wounds of the Lord Jesus in his heart just as later brilliantly appeared from the renewal of the same wounds in his body" (L3C 5.14). Francis had been confronted with the sweetness of the Lord on a night in Assisi's streets, and, as he recalls in his *Testament*, that same sweetness came to him when he served the lepers, the sight of whom he had formerly found bitter. Now the bitter sweetness of Christ's passion impressed itself upon his memory and began to shape his prayer and activity.

He would repair San Damiano. He needed materials and funds. He went to Foligno and sold everything he had, hoping to use the money for the little church. Francis's father discovered his intentions and maneuvered to get the money (and perhaps his son) back. As we know, the two ended up before the bishop of Assisi and parted ways for good. At that moment, Francis made public to Assisi the break he had already made with "the age" the day he kissed a leper's hand. A new life was taking shape. "Returning to the church of San Damiano, joyful and eager" after the confrontation with his father, "he made a hermit's habit.... Then getting up and going back to the city, he began to praise the Lord throughout the piazzas and neighborhoods, like one inebriated in the Spirit." Francis's Spirit-filled praise prepared him to make a request: "When he finished praising the Lord in this way, he turned to obtaining stones for the repair of the church. 'Whoever gives me one stone,' he would say, 'will have one reward. Whoever gives me two will have two rewards'" (L3C 7.21).

We can only imagine how crazy this must have looked. Here comes Francis, chugging up the steep hill from San Damiano, perhaps with a cart, perhaps with just his own two hands. All the people he passed knew him and knew what had recently transpired between Francis and his father. They used to hear him with his friends, singing songs in the streets after a rowdy feast. Now he's singing about God and asking for stones to rebuild a church no one cares about. What a fool! But Francis seems to have answered any abuse he suffered with patience and joy, simply asking for more stones. He got those stones from bewildered and charmed townspeople, hoisted them on his shoulders and headed back down the hill to San Damiano, singing. Soon he would return, begging door to door not only for more stones but for food, banqueting on a pile of slop in a bowl he carried (L3C 7.22). When he wasn't hungry, he begged for oil to keep the light burning before the cross in that decrepit church. He begged for the lepers too, and he kept singing. None of this was easy. Francis had to set aside his pride and humble himself to ask for these things from people who knew him, who knew who he *was*. He ran into his father routinely, who was embarrassed at the sight of Francis and cursed him. But he kept working hard on little San Damiano, concentrating on the thing right before his face.

Then the Letter came to Francis in a new way, and Francis, who always wanted more, embraced the more the Spirit gave him. While at Mass one day he heard the Gospel "to carry no *gold or silver, a wallet or a purse, bread, walking stick or shoes or two tunics.*" He talked to the priest to make sure he understood the Latin words correctly and then couldn't contain himself: "This is what I want to do with all my strength!" (*L3C* 8.25). He committed himself to an even deeper poverty, wore even rougher clothes, fasted while he worked, and exhorted others to do penance in simple words. As he remembered in his *Testament*, he also began to greet people differently; "May the Lord give you his peace" (*L3C* 8.26; *Test* 23), he said, coming up the hill for more stones. This peace became his constant message as he exhorted fellow citizens to penance and the Gospel, as he worked, as he begged, as he tended to lepers. He seemed to know the peace he offered despite how evidently he suffered, a suffering he had chosen because he wished to do penance.

The peace that Francis announced, the Lord's peace, slowly crept through Assisi. Like Nicodemus, Bernard of Quintavalle visited Francis in secret at San Damiano. Bernard eventually invited Francis to his house for dinner and made his intentions clear: he wanted to give all his wealth and possessions away and join Francis. So did Peter, another man from Assisi. The Spirit was creating something new. Francis recognized clearly what they needed to do—consult the Letter:

Rising at daybreak...they went to the church of Saint Nicholas, next to the piazza of the city of Assisi. They entered for prayer, but, because they were simple, they did not know how to find the passage in the Gospel about renunciation of the age [*saeculi*]. They prayed devoutly that the Lord would show them his will on opening the book the first time. When the prayer was finished, blessed Francis took the closed book, and kneeling before the altar, opened it....The Lord's counsel confronted them: *If you wish to be perfect, go sell everything you possess and give it to the poor, and you will have a treasure in heaven.* (Mark 10:21; L3C 8.29)

They opened this Gospel book (now preserved at the Walters Art Museum in Baltimore, Maryland) two more times, in honor of the Trinity, and found more poverty, more denial, more penance. Francis said to Bernard and Peter: "Brothers, this is our life and rule....Go and fulfill what you have heard" (L3C 8.29). Not long after this event, two more brothers joined them. Francis was moved to try something else: "'We are to go throughout the world,' he explained, 'encouraging everyone, more by deed than by word, to do penance for their sins and to recall the commandments of God'" (L3C 10.36). He knew this wouldn't be easy. He gave them words of comfort: "With confidence simply proclaim penance, trusting in the Lord who conquered the world, that by his Spirit he is speaking through and in you, exhorting everyone to come back to him and follow his commandments" (L3C 10.36).

The brothers left for different places. They needed Francis's words ringing in their heads. People didn't understand who they were or what they wanted. The peace the brothers gave in greeting was often met with scorn, beatings, and humiliation, but the brothers did not strike back. When they spoke, it was of peace and penance. They knew their efforts required the Spirit's aid, and so "According to the word of the Gospel, they prayed with care and fervor [*sollicite et ferventer*] for their persecutors" (*L3C* 10.40). Before long, some who abused them turned back to them for forgiveness. The brothers' commitment to the Letter in their speech and in their bodies gave the Spirit a place to move. Peace and reconciliation followed.

Time passed. The brothers kept living the life they discovered in the Letter of the Gospel. They lived in poverty, sharing the little they possessed. They attended Mass together, prayed together, worked together, did penance together, and encouraged others to penance. They announced peace. The love they had for each other and the Lord they followed was as obvious as the difficulty of the life they chose. Around 1209 Francis and eleven brothers decided to take the outline for their way of life, consisting mainly of scriptural quotations, to Rome for approval by the pope. This early outline, called the *propositum vitae*, is now totally lost to us, but different stories relate the central point: with the aid of churchmen and the Spirit, the group from Assisi received approval for their Gospel life. They also received tonsure, a haircut marking their place in the Church and world, and a commission to preach the Gospel. They hadn't sought tonsure or preaching but responded faithfully to what the Spirit gave them.

Returning to Assisi from Rome, they eventually centered life around the Church of St. Mary of the Angels, the Portiuncula, another church Francis had repaired. The first church that he repaired, San Damiano, soon had inhabitants. On the night of Palm Sunday 1211, spurred on by conversations with Francis about the Gospel life, a young noblewoman named Clare fled her home and the city of Assisi and stole down the hill and through the plain to the Portiuncula.

The brothers met her and cut her hair to signify her embrace of a new life. Francis then took her to a nearby religious community. Clare did not stay long. The Letter of the Gospel had cut her open, and the Spirit stirred her to keep moving until she settled at San Damiano. There she stayed, praying and working, leading a life uniquely configured to the poverty of the Gospel she desired. Her commitment was as powerful and magnetic as Francis's own, and a community of women soon gathered around her and spread across Europe.

Francis, Clare, and the brothers and sisters that joined them had made a stunning choice to leave behind a stable, comfortable life for the instability and difficulties of a Gospel life lived in the world. Filled with love to follow Christ, they refused ownership, authority, money, status, and power. As time passed, Francis and the brothers continued to develop a document that expressed their life. This document is called the Earlier Rule or Rule without a Papal Seal. The Later Rule, which was approved by the pope in 1223, is much briefer. If we take up the Earlier Rule, we can gain further insight into the life these brothers led.

The Rule begins with a prayerful oath: "In the name of the Father and of the Son and the Holy Spirit" (ER Prologue, 1). The next words are, "This is the life...." Like any religious community, the Rule these brothers wish to observe is not just a code of conduct but living Letters animated by the Spirit. The first chapter of the Rule begins to spell out their life: "The Rule and Life of these brothers is this, namely to live in obedience, in chastity, and without anything of their own and to follow the teaching and footprints of our Lord Jesus Christ" (ER 1.1). Like other religious communities, they sought to imitate Christ through these vows, being obedient to authorities inside and outside their community, refusing marriage, and owning nothing. With these vows, Francis and the early brothers lived poverty in a way that went beyond what most religious communities meant by the term. Typically speaking, poverty for a monastic community meant that things were owned in common. In this way, a monastery could become quite rich though each individual member would still be "poor," since each individual owned nothing.

By contrast, Francis and the brothers of the early community wanted to own nothing at all, and what they did have out of necessity (like their own clothes and a few liturgical books), they wanted to be of little value. The brothers' poverty meant they kept no food for the next day and had to obtain food and other necessities by their daily labor. They refused money as payment, which would have given them security and separated them from those they wished to serve. If they were given nothing at all for their labor, they would beg. Adding to their insecurity, the brothers refused ownership of the places where they lived (like the Portiuncula). They often lived or stayed in churches or with the poor and needy, even lepers.

Francis's and his brothers' commitment to poverty was not animated by trying to outdo other religious communities. Their commitment to the vows they took flowed from the promise that they made in the opening lines of the Rule "to follow the teaching [*doctrina*] and footprints [*vestigia*] of our Lord Jesus Christ." We should further reflect on this promise. Someone's teaching is something we read or hear about. We are passive before it; we receive it. This is good. We need to listen to those who know. Francis and his brothers want to listen to the Letter, the teaching of Christ. They listened to Christ in the Earlier Rule itself, which grounds what they do in scriptural verses. Francis's "Admonitions" were another way to hear and ponder Christ's teaching. Francis's life of prayer, particularly the saying of the Office(s), which he demands of all the literate and clerical brothers, is another way of listening to the *doctrina Christi*. What has been heard must also be done; hearing must flow into following, and following sharpens hearing. While following Christ's teaching can amount to studying the Scriptures and trying later to practice what is read, trying to follow Christ's footprints is much different. We can only follow footprints by getting up and walking. If we want to follow the footprints well, we must walk carefully and deliberately, like a child following a parent in the snow. If the child gets too silly or tries to go too fast, the child will miss the footprint, stumble, and fall. The careful, patient, deliberate child will find each footprint and travel easily. If the child follows well, the parent's footprints will appear clearest in the snow; there will be no sign of the child's own steps. So, too, with following Christ. When done with the Spirit it will seem that only Christ has been there, the very thing the servant of Christ desires.

The Earlier Rule offers various images of Jesus whose footprints the brothers follow, but one image is central: Jesus washing the feet of the apostles at the Last Supper. This image of Jesus is present in many places, explicitly and implicitly, in the Earlier Rule. One explicit place is chapter 6. This brief chapter indicates that brothers who feel they cannot live the Rule must go immediately to their minister, a brother put in place to help with just these kinds of situations. The minister must try to provide for the brother just as he would hope to have someone do for him if he were in similar straits (ER 6, 2). The chapter concludes by saying, "Let no one be called 'prior,' but let everyone in general be called a lesser brother. Let one wash the feet of the other" (ER 6, 3). The last words are a clear reference to John 13, where Jesus takes a towel and bowl and washes the feet of the apostles. This is the Jesus whom the brothers, especially the brothers in positions of authority, are instructed to imagine themselves to be. Francis makes this clear in the fourth of his "Admonitions," which begins, "*I did not come to be served but to serve* says the Lord (Matt 20:28). Let those who are placed over others boast about that position as much as they would if they were assigned the duty of washing the feet of their brothers" (Adm 4.1–2). This admonition concludes with a warning: "And if they are more upset at having their place over others taken away from them than at losing their position at their feet, the more they store up a *money bag* to the peril of their soul" (John 12:6; Adm 4.3). A brother should only care about losing a position of power if the brother has first understood that he is losing the opportunity to wash the brothers' feet. If he expresses any other attitude, he doesn't really care about his poor brothers but about the coins in the *money bag* of his own power; he becomes Judas.

Chapter 6 of the Earlier Rule also shows that all the brothers must bear this attitude of foot washer because this action glosses or explains the name the brothers take—*fratres minores*, or "lesser brothers." We usually call the brothers of this religious order "Franciscans," after their founder, but the name they chose signifies much more. *Fratres minores* links them to the image of Jesus washing the feet of his brothers on the night before he died. This Jesus, the Master who serves and is about to die, is therefore always before them. Francis would connect this image to all the names of positions within the order. So, rather than use a term like *prior*, which means "before," Francis chose the name *custos* for the brother who watches over the affairs of a community, a word that gives us "custodian." He is a person who serves, who looks out for others, and is not placed before anyone. Likewise, the head of the entire order is called the "minister general," a name clearly reflecting service.

As scholars have long pointed out, *fratres minores* is also a name loaded with cultural meaning. In Francis's time and place, society was stratified into *maiores* and *minores*—greater and lesser. These terms could distinguish broad groups, like the rich from the poor. *Maiores* and *minores* could also be applied to groups like the nobility to distinguish greater (or more important) nobles from lesser ones, or to distinguish greater and lesser merchants, and so on. Francis therefore consciously chose to be a *frater minor*, someone lesser, who identified with all those who were unimportant, poor, and powerless. As he remembered in his *Testament*: "we were simple and subject to all" (*Test* 19). The brothers made themselves servants and subjects of all whom they encountered. This is a stunning choice. We must remember that in the Middle Ages, an abbot (the head of a monastic community), a bishop, or the priest of a wealthy church, was a civic leader, a person who had power and wealth. Francis and his brothers had the right to claim power and authority but wanted none, and rather than *say* that other church people should divest themselves of their wealth and power in imitation of Christ, they *did* it.

Chapter 7 of the Earlier Rule shows us one way the brothers divested themselves of authority and power. The chapter specifies that the brothers must work but that they cannot take positions of authority where they work, nor can they handle or receive money. So, if a brother is on a work site, using the carpenter's trade he knew before he became a lesser brother, he cannot be the "foreman." Instead, the brother must be a day laborer, taking only lunch for his wages. Similarly, if a brother is working in a house of charity, he cannot be the person directing the activity, or determining who gets alms; he must go out and beg or stay in the house and minister to the sick and needy. The brothers must always be "the lesser ones and be subject to all" (ER 7, 2) and go about this task joyfully (ER 7, 15). They also displayed their commitment to being lesser in the poor clothes they wore and the way they traveled—on foot, rather than on horseback (unless need demanded it) (ER 2, 13–14, 15).

In their work and daily activity, the brothers aimed to be lesser, to be foot washers. In this way they strove to display the same humility of Jesus that they saw in the Gospels, that indeed they saw at every liturgy as Jesus came to them humbly in his body and blood through the hands of a priest. They were embracing the Letter of the Gospel with their lives, just as each day they surrounded themselves with God's Letters in prayer. Francis worked, prayed, and exhorted himself and others to penance. In addition to those exhortations to penance, Francis also preached, perhaps primarily because the Church had commissioned him to do so. He had no formal training in preaching. He relied on his life and prayer to inform his preaching. Two stories of Francis's preaching deserve our reflection.

In 1219, Francis made his way to Damietta, Egypt, where the Fifth Crusade was underway. Preparations for this crusade began in 1213, with a letter by Innocent III to the whole Church and continued in documents issued at one of the most important ecumenical councils of the Middle Ages, Lateran IV, in 1215. The pope called every single person to participate in the crusade in some way—through prayer and fasting, supporting crusaders with arms and goods, or "taking up the cross" and marching east. The liturgy itself was called upon to participate, as a new prayer was inserted into the Mass, pleading for the relief of the Holy Land. In short, one could not miss the preparations for this crusade, just as one could not avoid hearing tales of prior crusades.

In 1212, Francis twice attempted to go to Muslim occupied places and preach, but the ships never made their destinations. The winds favored Francis in 1219. When he arrived at Damietta after a long land and sea journey, the crusaders had already besieged the city. According to one medieval chronicle, Francis immediately sought out the cardinal legate in charge (Pelagius of Albano) and begged permission to preach to the sultan (*FA:ED* 1:605–6). The cardinal eventually agreed, but given the political situation, told Francis "that they were not to let anyone think that he [the cardinal] had sent them" (*FA:ED* 1:606). Francis and a companion walked in the direction of the sultan's camp. Most sources report that they were soon captured and eventually brought before the sultan, al-Kamil, with whom they remained for some days, preaching in his presence.

Francis knew the risk he took when he headed to the sultan's camp. He was as ready for this risk as he could be. Chapter 16 of the Earlier Rule displays the approach of Francis and his brothers to mission work and thus may capture Francis's attitude as he walked toward the sultan's camp. As usual, the chapter opens with Scripture: "The Lord says: *Behold I am sending you like sheep in the midst of wolves.* Therefore be *prudent as serpents and simple as doves*" (ER 16, 1; Matt 10:16). The Earlier Rule then offers two options for those who have received permission from their minister and wish to go "and live spiritually among the Saracens [that is, Muslims] and non-believers" (ER 16, 5). Each way reflects the prudence and simplicity Francis saw in the Gospel. "One way is not to engage in arguments or disputes but to be subject *to every human creature for God's sake* and to acknowledge that they [that is, the brothers] are Christians" (ER 16, 6). This mission path is no different from the life the brothers have already promised to live. For they have promised to be lesser brothers, foot washers and subject to others, in imitation of the Lord himself at the Last Supper. Among those they may fear as enemies, they will discover new depths of being lesser.

Francis's second way takes a different strategy. "The other way is to announce the Word of God, when they see it pleases the Lord, in order that they may believe in almighty

God, the Father, the Son and the Holy Spirit, the Creator of all, the Son the Redeemer and Savior and be baptized and become Christians" (ER 16, 7). This path stresses being attentive to the Spirit in the moment and making a simple announcement. The first path is not forgotten in this second one, since the lesser brother is still not encouraged to argue or dispute, but in this case the witness of life becomes a witness also in speech. Each path requires discernment, humility, and risk.

The Rule clarifies later in chapter 16 that all the brothers must commit themselves to this risk in their daily lives: "Wherever they may be, let all my brothers remember that they have given themselves and abandoned their bodies to the Lord Jesus Christ. For love of Him, they must make themselves vulnerable to their enemies, both visible and invisible" (ER 16, 10–11). When caring for lepers, when caring for each other, at prayer, at work, traveling, or at a mountain retreat, the brothers must offer themselves, whole and entire, body and soul. In this way they are stepping right inside the footprints of Jesus, who out of the depth of his love once suffered death to save us and who, now deathless, offers himself daily to sustain us.

As we saw in the *Testament* and in other texts, Francis had a deeply physical and literal view of his Christian faith. God communicates to us through bodies, through spaces, through things, and through written words. We return that communication to God by offering ourselves through our own bodies, risking pain and death. It is terrifying to be vulnerable in the face of violence, even potential violence, as Francis remembered every day as he prayed his Office of the Passion. Francis probably recognized that he might die if he made it before the sultan. He was ready to follow even this footprint of Jesus. Pursuing his second way, he determined that the Spirit wished him to voice the truth of Christian faith before the sultan. As Francis preached, he must have radiated the humility he saw in Jesus, living at this moment his prayer to love his neighbor "by giving offense to no one" (PrOF 5). Al-Kamil noticed; he was taken with Francis and listened to him. Most sources indicate that after some days, and seeing no clear end in sight, Francis and his companion indicated that they wanted to go back to the Christian camp. The same sources report that the sultan offered them various gifts to take but they refused. Al-Kamil was further impressed. Making sure they were well fed, he ensured their safe return to the camp (FA:ED 1:607).

In this dramatic episode of Francis's preaching, we see the depth of his commitment to the letter of the Gospel as he steps inside the footprint of Christ's offering of himself. Francis did this in such a humble way that the result was a peaceful encounter amid violence and war. This encounter focuses on where Jesus is headed—to his humiliating and saving death. Another episode of Francis's preaching reflects on Jesus's humble and saving birth.

In 1223, Francis made his way to the town of Greccio, Italy (about 55 miles south of Assisi), to celebrate Christmas. His particular love for this feast caused others to take notice because culturally Christmas did not have the standing in the medieval world that it does in ours. One text says of Francis's devotion to Christmas:

> Blessed Francis held the Nativity of the Lord in greater reverence than any other of the Lord's solemnities. For although the Lord may have accomplished our salvation in his other solemnities, nevertheless, once he was born to us, as blessed Francis would say, it was certain that we would be saved. On that day he wanted every Christian to rejoice in the Lord and, for love of

him who gave himself to us, wished everyone to
be cheerfully generous not only to the poor but
also to the animals and birds. (*AC* 14)

Another source tells how one year, Christmas fell on a Friday,
and the brothers argued over whether or not they should eat
meat, since at that time abstaining from meat on every Friday
was the standard expectation. Francis weighed in: "You sin,
brother, when you call 'Friday' the day when *unto us a Child is
born*. I want even the walls to eat meat on that day" (2C 199).
Christmas was a feast, not a "Friday." Meat would be served.

Perhaps an even clearer sign of Francis's devotion to
Christmas is the way he modified his Office of the Passion
to celebrate it. For Christmas and its season Francis composed a specific psalm that he prayed at multiple hours of
the day. The psalm begins with a joyful shout: "Exult in God
our help! Shout to the Lord God living and true with cries
of gladness....Because the most holy Father of heaven, our
king before all ages, sent his beloved Son from on high and
he was born of the Blessed Virgin holy Mary" (OfP 15, 1–3;
FA:ED 1:156). The hinge of the Psalm concentrates specifically on Christ's birth and its conditions: "For the most holy
beloved child has been given to us and has been born for us
on the way and placed in a manger because he did not have
a place in the inn" (OfP 15, 7; *FA:ED* 1:156). More joyful
praise follows until Francis jars the reader with the implica-
tions of Christ's humble presence among us in the last line
of the psalm: "Take up your bodies and carry his holy cross
and follow his most holy commands to the end" (OfP 15, 13;
FA:ED 1:157). The tenderness of Christmas hearkens to the
cross.

No one describes Christmas at Greccio in 1223 with
more depth of feeling and theological insight than Thomas
of Celano, and so we will follow his portrayal of events. This

story of Christmas is the conclusion to the first and longest part of Thomas's *Life of Saint Francis*. He prefaces the story of Greccio with a summary of how he views Francis at this point in his life. His summary is worthy of meditation:

> His highest aim, foremost desire, and greatest intention was to pay heed to the holy Gospel in all things and through all things, to follow the teaching of our Lord Jesus Christ and to imitate his footsteps completely with all vigilance and all zeal, all the desire of his soul and all the fervor of his heart. Francis used to recall with regular meditation the words of Christ and recollect his deeds with most attentive perception. Indeed, so thoroughly did the humility of the Incarnation and the charity of the Passion occupy his memory that he scarcely wanted to think of anything else. (1C 84)

Here, Thomas displays Francis as a committed follower of his own Gospel rule. He singles out Francis's focus on the humility of the incarnation and the charity of the passion. We know how true this is. Francis centered his mind on the memory of Christ's passion in his daily prayer and saw God's humility at every celebration of the Mass. The sea of God's love and humility that occupied his memory flowed in and out of his life of work and prayer to the point that he would risk his life to follow and announce the teaching and footprints of Jesus Christ. Now, at Greccio, he would place before himself and all gathered for Christmas worship the footprint of Christ's humility in a new and unforgettable way.

Thomas of Celano relates that Francis asked a friend from Greccio named John to make specific preparations for this celebration of Christmas. "For I wish to enact," Francis instructed John, "the memory of that babe who was born in Bethlehem: to see as much as is possible with my own bodily eyes the discomfort of his infant needs, how he lay in a manger, and how with an ox and an ass standing by, he rested on hay" (1C 30, 84). As we have seen many times, for Francis the physical mediates the spiritual. Francis wants to behold the scene of Jesus's birth with his own two eyes in order to reinforce the memory in his mind's eye. He wants a real, living, nativity scene set to the words of Luke 2 and Isaiah 1:3. He wants to see the Letter, and he wants others to see it as well.

On Christmas night, John has prepared the scene just as Francis wished. Thomas of Celano casts his eyes over the setting: "Indeed the manger is prepared, the hay is carried in, and the ox and the ass are led to the spot. There simplicity is given a place of honor, poverty is exalted, humility is commended, and out of Greccio is made a new Bethlehem." As the people of Greccio approach, Thomas observes that "they rejoice with new joy [*novis gaudiis adlaetantur*] at this new mystery." Even the priest, celebrating the liturgy over the manger, "enjoys a new consolation." Francis himself "stands before the manger, filled with heartfelt sighs, contrite in his piety, and overcome with wondrous joy" (1C 30, 85). Immersed in this joy, with the live nativity scene in view, Francis sings the Gospel and begins to preach. Thomas presents Francis as a moving and tender preacher, overcome with love himself when he says the words "Jesus" or "child of Bethlehem." He seems not just to speak these words but to taste their sweetness (1C 30, 86). Thomas says that as the night moves on, a man has a vision of a lifeless child lying in the manger. Francis approaches and stirs the child as if it had been in a deep sleep. "Nor is this vision unfitting," Thomas reflects, "since in the hearts of many the child Jesus has been given over to oblivion. Now he is awakened and impressed on their loving memory by his own grace through his holy servant Francis" (1C 30, 86).

Francis believed that he and the people of Greccio needed to see a physical representation of the manger, so they could see right before their faces the humble poverty of Jesus. This was the same humility he saw at the liturgy, that he attempted to live, that animated his Rule. When the people of Greccio and their priest saw the scene that Francis and John had prepared, they felt as though they were seeing a new mystery, reading a new Letter. Francis believed that the clear sight of the Letter could stir the cool embers of the mind and heart. The Letter, seen with the Spirit, can pull any one of us from conformity to this age and its forgetfulness into conformity with the living memory the Eternal Father desires each of us to have—the memory of his beloved Son.

5

La Verna/*Alverna*

La Verna is a desert but not a place full of sand. *Desert*, following the Latin, signifies any uninhabited place. *Desert* can also mean a "hermitage," a place of solitude, where the land's quiet opens up the pilgrim's interior spaces. The desert of La Verna is remote and cold, even in the summer.

La Verna is a mountain but not a snow-covered peak. The mountain of La Verna is thickly wooded. At one point in the ascent, great rocks, torn by fissures, mark the pilgrim's path. The mountain of La Verna is high and hard.

When Francis took the steep path up La Verna for the last time in August of 1224, he headed there with purpose. According to one source, he explained to a companion, "I want to make a 'Lent' here, in honor of God, the Blessed Virgin Mary, His mother, and Blessed Michael, the prince of angels and of souls" (AC 118). La Verna was much simpler, much rougher, when Francis made his "Lent." Now, upon the rock plateau and in the surrounding woods, churches and chapels, a convent, and buildings to house pilgrims dot the mountainside. In 1224, perhaps only small huts and a very rustic chapel existed. Near where those huts once stood, deep crevices split the rock of La Verna and formed hollows and caves. One formation called Sasso Spico creates a great canopy of overhanging rock. Francis descended into those dark places for prayer. He also prayed atop the plateau, where he could behold the sweep of God's creation. He especially liked to cross to the other side of the rock, reachable then only by a log laid across a fissure. Now, you can walk through a corridor across that same fissure to a series of chapels whose walls rise from the very edge of the cliff. La Verna is a stunning and challenging place, suited to penance and prayer.

The Francis who fasted and prayed upon La Verna in 1224 was different from his younger self. Francis first went to La Verna around 1213, when Orlando di Chiusi granted the mountain to him as a place of retreat. By 1224, Francis was seriously ill. Historians explain that Francis had contracted a form of malaria from the East that affected his liver and gave him frequent fevers. He had also contracted a form of conjunctivitis that caused his eyes serious pain and robbed him more and more of his sight. The treatments for his eyes were as bad as the effects of the disease. One story tells that Francis and some brothers traveled to the hermitage of Fonte Colombo to see a physician. The doctor arrived from nearby Rieti with instruments of healing—an iron poker to be heated in the fire, to cauterize Francis's face from jaw to eyebrow. As the doctor prepared for the procedure, Francis addressed the fire and prayed, "My Brother Fire, noble and useful among all the creatures the Most High created, be courtly to me in this hour. For a long time, I have loved you and I still love you for the love of that Lord who created you. I pray our Creator who made you, to temper your heat now, so that I may bear it." Francis then blessed the fire with the Sign of the Cross. His brothers left the room, unable to watch. When they came back, Francis consoled them: "Why did you run away? I tell you the truth: I felt no pain or even heat from the fire. In fact, if it's not well cooked, cook it some more" (AC 86). The doctor was amazed. Of course, the treatment did nothing to help Francis as the brothers noted and as other doctors at the time had warned. So, another physician pierced his ears.

In 1224, Francis also had a different relationship to the Order of Lesser Brothers. In 1220, to the surprise of all, Francis resigned from his position of leadership as the head of the order. His resignation may have been animated by various factors, including his poor health and his own perception of what would keep the growing order tied to the Gospel life of the Rule. He suffered through his illnesses and his resignation.

Different stories tell of life on La Verna, either in relation to Francis's final visit or in relation to others. If Francis and his brothers followed the Rule for Hermitages, then we can assume that saying the Office structured their days and nights on the mountain. Most stories suggest, however, that Francis became deeply reclusive. Perhaps he prayed alone for days at a time, using the Offices that he typically prayed, delving further into the Letter and the Spirit that animates them. Perhaps he spent much of his time in silence. In accordance with the Rule and the stories of La Verna, we can reason that Francis had at least one companion to take care of him upon the mountain, or as the Rule for Hermitages termed it, a mother. That mother was probably Brother Leo. At the least, Brother Leo was on La Verna with Francis in 1224, helping Francis keep the fast. Brother Leo was originally from Assisi, and he would die there in 1278, long after Francis. He was Francis's confessor, one of his closest brothers in religion, and sometimes he acted as his scribe. He kept something precious in the folds of his habit from that last visit to La Verna, an old piece of parchment from Francis himself.

One story of La Verna tells us that a brother came to Francis's cell to read him the Gospel of the day before dinner, a custom Francis observed when he couldn't hear Mass. From this we can see that Francis always stayed close to the rhythms of the liturgy, even when he could not or did not attend worship. Before the brother had left to read Francis the Gospel, the brother had lit a fire in his own cell. When he and Francis returned, the fire was crawling up the whole structure. They needed immediate help. "But Blessed Francis," the story tells, "did not want to help [the brother]: he took the hide that he used to cover himself at night and went into the forest." Some brothers hurried over and helped to put out the fire. Francis later came back to eat and said after the meal, "From now on I don't want this hide over me since because of my avarice I did not want Brother Fire to consume it" (AC 87).

We may react to Francis's words and actions here with confusion, amusement, or anger. We are not told how the brothers on the mountain reacted. Francis's perspective is clear. He had not acted as a Lesser Brother. He wanted something of his own, a piece of hide, but had promised to live *sine proprio*—without anything of his own. He strove to be subject to all but refused to be subject to Brother Fire, who had been pliant to his prayers. He had promised to offer his body to Jesus Christ and to make himself vulnerable to enemies seen and unseen but would not risk his blanket. This meant that he also refused to help his brothers in need upon the mountain. Accordingly, he rid himself of the hide.

Thomas of Celano narrates the key events at La Verna in 1224 in the second "book" of his *Life of Saint Francis*. He was the first to write of this event (rather than the likely inauthentic "Letter of Brother Elias"), and Thomas's account informs all subsequent descriptions. This section of Thomas's *Life of Saint Francis* opens with an announcement of Francis's death and another summation of Francis's life and virtues. A story follows this summary, which sets the stage for Thomas's presentation of La Verna. Thomas relates that Francis, as he did many times, went to a place of rest and solitude for deep prayer. "After he had been there" in this unnamed place "for some time, through unceasing prayer and frequent contemplation, he reached intimacy with God in an indescribable way" (1C 91). Thomas uses the word *familiaritas* to name Francis's intimacy, a word medieval theologians used to describe Moses's relationship to God, or how Jesus in his human nature relates to the Father, or even the Divine Word's intimacy with the Father. In this tender space of prayer, Francis speaks to God:

> He wanted [*cupiebat*] to know what in him and about him was or could be more acceptable [*acceptius*] to the eternal King. With utmost diligence [*curiosissime*] he sought and with total devotion [*piissime*] he longed to know in what manner, on what path [*via*], and with what desire he could cling more perfectly to the Lord God, according to the counsel and good pleasure of God's will. (1C 91)

From the depths of his intimacy with God, Francis recognizes his profound distance from God and desires to close the gap. He knows, however, that the "more" he desires can only come if it is in accord with the will of the one whom he desires. In other words, Francis wants precisely that nearness that God wants to give him and desires it in the manner that God wishes to give it. Francis has therefore reached a yet more intimate stage in his life with God, confirmed by what happens next: "Then he felt pouring down on him from above a sweetness and delight rarely given to even a few, and it made him lose himself completely." Thomas then continues, "This man, having the spirit of God, was ready to endure any suffering of the mind and bear any affliction of the body, if at last the *optio* would be given to him so that the will of the heavenly Father might be fulfilled mercifully in him" (1C 92).

The Latin word *optio* can mean choice. *Optio* also means an assistant. If we allow this meaning, we can see that Francis is willing to receive any aid God chooses to give him so that he may enter more fully into God in accordance with the prayer he has just made. Francis believed that this aid would be revealed to him in the Letters of the Gospel. And so, filled with the Spirit, Francis went into the chapel of the hermitage and put the Book of the Gospels on the altar. "Then he prostrated himself with his heart as much as his body in prayer to God, asking in humble prayer that God...be pleased to show him his will...at the first opening of the book" (1C 92). Francis made the Sign of the Cross and opened the Gospels. In the quiet, his eyes found a passage telling of Christ's passion, of the suffering he would endure. Francis cracked the Gospels two more times. "Every time he found either the same text or one that was similar" (1C 93). A general truth of Christian life suddenly became immediate to Francis: "The man full of the Spirit of God then understood that he would have to enter into the kingdom of God through many trials, through many difficulties, and through many struggles" (1C 93).

Thomas's description of Francis as a *vir Spiritu Dei plenus* (a man full of the Spirit of God) relates to at least one biblical passage, as editors and translators have noted. In Genesis 41:38, Pharaoh says these words about Joseph after Joseph interprets his dreams and gives him counsel. We could find parallels between Joseph and Francis that Thomas might have intended and which might illuminate Thomas's description of these events. If we allow that the Spirit of God can also mean the Holy Spirit, then further connections can be made. In the

Acts of the Apostles, at least two men are described as *plenus Spiritu Sancto*: Stephen (7:55) and Barnabas (11:24). In the case of Stephen, he is said to be full of the Holy Spirit before he proclaims his faith and undergoes his death. Thomas would surely approve of us connecting Stephen to Francis. A different verse, however, presents a connection with Christ himself. In Luke 4:1, Jesus is described as *plenus Spirtu Sancto* after his baptism, when he leaves the Jordan and the Spirit drives him into the desert, to a place of fasting, solitude, and prayer. Thomas presents Francis in a similar light; he is filled with the Spirit of God and is ready to be driven into the desert. While Christ's forty-day fast occurs at the beginning of his ministry, Francis's critical fast occurs at the end; and while Christ's fast culminates in an encounter with the accuser, a fallen angel bent on humanity's ruin, Francis's fast culminates in an entirely different angelic encounter.

August became September. Perhaps it was near the middle of September, near the Feast of the Exaltation of the Cross, that Francis crossed the flat rock of La Verna, crossed the fissure carved into the mountain, and began to pray on the other side. We must allow Thomas of Celano to tell us what happened next.

> He [Francis] saw in the vision of God a man, like a six-winged Seraph, standing above him, arms extended and feet joined, affixed to a cross. Two wings were above his head, two were stretched out to fly, and two covered his whole body. When the blessed servant of the most High saw these things, he was filled with the greatest awe, but he did not know what this vision meant for him. He greatly rejoiced too and was much delighted by the kind and gracious look that he saw the Seraph gave him, whose beauty was beyond reckoning, but the

fastening to the cross and the bitterness of the suffering sunk his spirits [*deterrebat*]. Consequently, he
got up both sad and happy as joy and sorrow took
their turns in him. Concerned over the matter, he
kept thinking about what this vision could mean
and his spirit was very anxious to capture an intelligible meaning from the vision. (1C 94)

Francis's search for intelligible meaning had no time to prog-
ress. Thomas continues:

At that moment when he could not perceive in
his mind anything clearly from the vision and the
newness of the vision pressed much upon his heart,
signs of the nails began to appear on his hands and
feet, just as he had seen them a little while earlier
on the crucified man above him. His hands and
feet seemed to be pierced through the middle by
nails, with the heads of the nails on the inner part
of his hands and on the upper part of his feet, and
their points protruding on opposite sides. Those
marks on the inside of his hands were round, but
rather oblong on the outside; and small pieces of
flesh were visible like the points of nails, bent over
and flattened, extending beyond the flesh around
them. On his feet, the marks of nails were stamped
in the same way and raised above the surrounding
flesh. His right side, as if pierced by a lance, had
a closed scar and often dripped blood, so that his
tunic and undergarments were frequently stained
with his holy blood. (1C 94–95)

Two mysteries face us, mysteries bound to bodies: Francis's vision and Francis's wounds. The mysteries face each other, like the ancient cherubim atop the mercy seat.

Deep in prayer upon the mountain, Francis begins to behold God. Whatever vision of God Francis has, the vision shifts to something more intelligible to a human mind in this life than the radiant splendor of the ineffable and totally spiritual God. The vision shifts to a body, a man, but the man is unlike any Francis has ever seen. This man is like a six-winged seraph and this seraph is fixed to a cross. One antithesis gives way to another in Francis's vision, like a ladder upon which he is ascending or perhaps descending. The vision of God who cannot be seen, who dwells in inaccessible light, gives way to a man who can be seen; the man gives further way to a seraph, an angelic spirit, who as a spirit cannot be seen and cannot suffer and yet this seraph is crucified. A body that cannot be seen, a body that cannot suffer, is seen and suffers. But what is this vision of, besides these antitheses, ascending and descending, there upon the altar top of La Verna? We must turn to the Letter of the Scriptures for guidance. The book of the Prophet Isaiah (6:1–4) says:

> In the year that King Uzziah died, I saw the Lord sitting on a throne, high and lofty; and the hem of his robe filled the temple. Seraphs were in attendance above him; each had six wings: with two they covered their faces, and with two they covered their feet, and with two they flew. And one called to another and said:
>
> "Holy, holy, holy is the LORD of hosts;
> the whole earth is full of his glory."

The seraphim are the highest order of angelic spirits. They have a chief purpose: to offer God unending worship. The seraphim are often depicted as totally swathed in flame, coals of incense burning brightly before the Lord of Hosts. We take up their voices and sound their cry when we sing the Sanctus at the liturgy. Francis's vision of a seraph can be understood, then, as a liturgical vision, a vision of God's worship by an angel of worship. However, Francis's vision is not simply of a seraph but a man like a seraph, fixed to a cross. Accordingly, the vision leads to Christ on the cross. For Jesus Christ, himself God and man, offers perfect worship, perfect sacrifice, in the offering of himself upon the cross. Indeed, "In the days of his flesh, Jesus offered up prayers and supplications, with loud cries and tears, to the one who was able to save him from death," as he cried out in the psalmist's words on the cross, "and he was heard because of his reverent submission" (Heb 5:7–8; see Mark 15:34). For, "when Christ came as a high priest of the good things that have come…he entered once for all into the Holy Place, not with the blood of goats and calves, but with his own blood, thus obtaining eternal redemption" (Heb 9:11–12). Therefore "through him," we can "continually offer a sacrifice of praise to God" (Heb 13:15). The sacrifice of praise we offer is the life of the Gospel; it is the saying of the Psalms; it is the eucharistic sacrifice and the life the Eucharist makes possible. Kneeling with Francis atop the rock of La Verna, the mountain's stones give way to another mountain, for we seem to "have come to Mount Zion and to the city of the living God, the heavenly Jerusalem, and to innumerable angels in festal gathering… and to Jesus, the mediator of a new covenant, and to the sprinkled blood that speaks a better word than the blood of Abel" (Heb 12:22–24). We see with Francis the sacrifice of God's only son, that one sacrifice, the one about which we say, "Almighty God, we pray that your angel may take this sacrifice to your altar in heaven."

What more can we say? Francis saw that sacrifice at which he had aimed his life, not as it was on Golgotha, a shameful death, but as we learn that it is through worship: the source of eternal salvation, the blazing sacrifice of the God-Man, Jesus Christ. Now, as we face the other mystery of La Verna, the mystery of Francis's wounds, we must look with the light of the mystery of Francis's vision, a vision of Christ's supreme act of worship, the worship we give at our altars. Francis himself began to ponder his vision but found it utterly elusive to his mind in that moment. How could he not find it dizzying, raised so aloft? But the vision's meaning did not elude his body. Signs of nails made of Francis's own flesh emerged in his hands and feet. A scar furrowed his side.

Francis was becoming what he beheld at the altar, for if we receive the body and blood of the Lord well, we become what we receive, for God wants us to be his sacrifice (see St. Augustine, Sermon 227). Indeed, we must "present" our "bodies as a living sacrifice, holy and pleasing to God" our "spiritual worship," not conforming ourselves to this age but offering ourselves to be transformed by the renewal of our minds (Rom 12:1–2). With his prayer and his life, Francis was making this sacrifice. "Holding back nothing of himself for himself," he had gone "to [Jesus] outside the camp, bear[ing] the abuse he endured," realizing that "here we have no lasting city, but we are looking for the city that is to come" (Heb 13:13–14). Francis became not world weary because of this truth but free: free to aid the leper because he could bear the Lord's reproach; free to rebuild San Damiano because he went outside the city gate; free to go to the sultan because here he had no lasting city; free, for he embraced the Letter of the Gospel and the one who is "the way, and the truth, and the life" (John 14:6). Now, his living body began to bear

Christ's passion: not Christ dead and taken down from the cross, but Christ alive, suffering, praying, and reigning from the cross. This is what it means here to be incorporated into Christ, to become his body. We do not yet enjoy the fruits of resurrection. Here and now in our flesh we complete "what is lacking in Christ's afflictions for the sake of his body, that is, the church" (Col 1:24). Our transformation lies in our conformity to Christ's sacrifice, which tempers us, widens us, and joins us to him. Grace indeed builds upon nature, but "our God is a consuming fire" (Heb 12:29).

The Spirit, who gives gifts to all, sealed Francis's body with the Letter of our transformation, the Letter he craved, the Letter that gave him joy. This Letter is the mystery hidden from ages past (Col 1:28) that makes all things clear: the death and resurrection of God's beloved. The mystery was there in Abel and Isaac and Joseph; in their fathers Adam and Abraham and Jacob; in their mothers Eve and Sarah and Rachel. In Christ this mystery lives and speaks. In Christ, this mystery becomes the Letter that we may embrace with the Spirit's power. *On the mountain of La Verna, the Spirit made of Francis a Letter.*

What could be the response to such a gift? Francis chose secrecy. Thomas of Celano relates that very few knew of or saw this witness in Francis's flesh while he was alive (1C 95–96). Francis kept the wounds covered and of them he only said, according to Thomas, "I have hidden your works in my heart to avoid any sin against you" (1C 96; Ps 119:11). However, one text can show us Francis's response to this gift. Brother Leo, as mentioned earlier, had kept a poor old piece of parchment from his last trip with Francis to La Verna. We will not know how often he took it out to read it, or what its presence said to him of his friend and brother, whom he outlived for perhaps fifty years. After Leo died, the parchment eventually became one of the relics kept by the Franciscan monastery attached to the Basilica in Assisi, the Sacro Convento. On the inside of the folded piece of parchment, Francis wrote a blessing for Brother Leo and drew a Tau cross (a *T*) coming out of the mouth of a figure at the bottom of the parchment. Leo clearly treasured these personal words of Francis to him. On the outside of the parchment, Francis wrote a list of praises, now almost completely faded away. If Leo had not written rubrics, passages in red ink on the old parchment explaining what the texts were, then we may have never known why Francis wrote these words. Of the blessing and the drawing, Leo wrote, "The blessed Francis wrote this blessing for me with his own hand. In a similar way he made with his own hand this sign TAU together with a head [*caput*]" (*FA:ED* 1:108). Of the praises, on the outside of the parchment, Leo said the following: "Two years before his death, the blessed Francis spent forty days on Mount La Verna." After describing the time frame of the fast, Leo continues, "And the Lord's hand was upon him. After the vision and the message of the seraph and the impression of Christ's stigmata upon his body, he composed these praises…in his own hand, thanking God for the kindness bestowed upon him" (*FA:ED* 1:108).

The text, now known as "The Praises of God," is nearly illegible, so worn is Leo's parchment, but scholars have carefully reconstructed the words. There are many ways to understand the text, but one thing is certain: it is a chain of simple praises. What Leo preserved is not so much a text of prayer but a moment of prayer. Francis is not teaching or recording or admonishing. In these praises, Francis is feverishly praying right before us on the mountain. The English translation below reflects the Latin closely: Francis repeats *Tu es* over and over again. For he speaks to God not as some distant force but as someone with whom he speaks on the mountain as though face-to-face—as an "I" to a "You." His spirit is drenched in praise, and he lets that praise be made. In these praises we are invited into the space of his prayer as he offers it. It is not planned or edited. It is a man, caught up in the Spirit, who can only light up his tongue with the glory of God. We only have these words because his friend kept them.

In the text that follows, there are numerous scriptural references. The first line expands upon Psalm 76:15, "You are the God who works wonders," and also recalls Psalm 97:1, which Francis uses as the beginning of the ninth psalm of his Office of the Passion: "Sing to the Lord a new song, because he has done wonders." While it is easy to identify the "wonders" Francis praises as what happened in his body on the mountain, we might further see it as an outpouring of praise for all that God has done in his life, which has received a new signature on La Verna. Francis seems to stammer out his praises, but it is the stammering of the Spirit. As he so often does, Francis names God *altissimus*, most high, he names God the Trinity, and he names God the highest good, as he did daily in his Office of the Passion. He also names God "living and true," words Francis used frequently to allude to Jesus present in the Eucharist. After those opening lines, the praises roll out of Francis's mouth, a psalmist caught in the intensity of praise, who has no words other than those that name and praise his beloved. However we decide to read the text, these are the words that came to Francis, there upon La Verna:

> You are the holy Lord God who does wonders. You are strong. You are great. You are the most high. You are the almighty. You holy Father, King of heaven and earth. You are three and one, the Lord God of Gods. You are the good, all good, the highest good, Lord God living and true. You are

love, charity. You are wisdom. You are humility. You are patience. You are beauty. You are security. You are rest. You are gladness and joy. You are our hope. You are justice and moderation. You are all things, our riches to sufficiency. You are beauty. You are meekness. You are protector. You are guardian and defender. You are strength. You are our refuge. You are our faith. You are our charity. You are all our sweetness. You are our eternal life, great and wonderful Lord, almighty God, merciful Savior. (PrsG, *FA:ED* 1:109)

6

Sister Death/*Sora nostra morte corporale*

"'Most High, all-powerful, good Lord,' Francis suddenly began, 'Yours are the praises, the glory and the honor and all blessing, To you alone, Most High, do they belong, and no human being is worthy to name you'" (CtC 1–2).

Sitting in front of a few brothers, one of them surely Leo, he must have looked like a leper; bandages crisscrossed parts of his body, scars traveled across his face from treatments for his eyes, his frame was wasted, his eyes cloudy and practically useless, only causing him pain. But there he sat, his mind clear, as he opened his mouth in a "new Praise of the Lord for his creatures," the text often called "The Canticle of Creatures" or "The Canticle of Brother Sun" (AC 83). The words streamed from him freely. This time, he did not focus on Christ in his passion, or in his victory, but on the creation Christ's victory transformed. This joyful praise did not stream from a healthy man gazing wide-eyed at each flower and blade of grass that he passed by but from a man who was

now enduring intense physical suffering and needed continual care.

For the last two years of his life, after he had come
down from La Verna for the last time, Francis was shipped
from doctor to doctor and place to place. More "treatments"
for his eyes, more attempts to cure his stomach and at each
place, the "prudent" brothers kept steering his steps closer
to Assisi, where they wanted him to be when he died. Now,
nearly at the end of his life, he was staying in a thatched hut
next to San Damiano. It was a horrible place—cold, drafty,
and crawling with mice. He "lay there for more than fifty
days," through the late winter, waiting to get more treatments, "unable" because of his eyes "to bear the light of the
sun during the day or the light of a fire at night" (AC 83).
When he forgot about the stabbing pain and the cold, the
mice ensured that he still couldn't sleep. Exhausted from all
these trials, one night "he was moved with piety for himself
and he said within himself," mimicking familiar words, "O
Lord, to help me, look upon my illnesses, so that I may be
able to bear them patiently" (AC 83). He was immediately
told in the spirit:

> What if, in exchange for your illnesses and trou-
> bles, someone were to give you a treasure? And it
> would be so great and precious that, even if the
> whole earth were changed to pure gold, all stones
> to precious ones, and all water to balsam, you would
> still judge and hold all these things as nothing...in
> comparison to the great and precious treasure given
> you. Wouldn't you greatly rejoice? (AC 83)

Francis agreed that he would. In the spirit he further heard:
"Then be glad and rejoice in your illnesses and troubles,
because as of now, you are as safe as if you were already in

my kingdom" (*AC* 83). In the morning, he spoke to his companions with his new clarity:

> I must rejoice greatly from now on in my illnesses and troubles and be consoled in the Lord, giving thanks always to God the Father, to his only Son our Lord Jesus Christ, and to the Holy Spirit for such a great grace and blessing—that while still living in the flesh he has deigned through his mercy to assure me, his unworthy little servant, of the kingdom. (*AC* 83)

In response to this new consolation, one he felt he didn't deserve, he wanted to offer something "for [the Lord's] praise, for our consolation and for the edification of our neighbor" (*AC* 83). He sat outside that terrible hovel by the church that he loved and broke out in a song of praise that no one had ever heard but which intoned familiar notes. He made his new praises in his own Umbrian language, not Latin. He set his praises to music and taught his brothers to sing them.

Francis's new song of praise resonated with the prayer or collect he composed for his Office of the Passion and with the spontaneous praises he made on La Verna, which he left to Brother Leo. Looking again at the first verses of the canticle, we see that it begins with Francis's typical mode of prayer: praise. "Most High, all powerful, good Lord, Yours are the praises, the glory and the honor and all blessing, To you alone, Most High, do they belong, and no one is worthy to name You" (*CtC* 1–2). Right before he says he has no right to speak of God is Francis's most typical way of naming God: God is highest (*altissimu*), all powerful (*omnipotente*), and good (*bon Signore*). What right have any of us, we who are of "unclean lips" (Isa 6:5), to speak of God? Not even an assurance of the kingdom could allow Francis a false intimacy with

God or peel his attention from the truth. He has no right to speak of the Highest. This recognition creates the space for praise. And so, out of the depth of his suffering, suffering so tied to his sight, Francis next praises the very part of creation that causes him the most pain:

> Praised be you my Lord with all your creatures, especially Sir Brother Sun, Who is the day and through whom you give us light. And he is beautiful and radiant with great splendor; and bears a likeness of you, Most High One. (CtC 3)

The sun's radiance stabs Francis's eyes. He offers praise. He then keeps praising those beautiful things that constitute the parameters and foundations of the universe as he knew it:

> Praised be You, my Lord, through Sister Moon and the stars, in heaven you made them clear and precious and beautiful.
> Praised be you, my Lord, through Brother Wind, and through the air, cloudy and serene, and every kind of weather, through whom you give sustenance to Your creatures.
> Praised be you, my Lord, through Sister Water, who is very useful and humble and precious and chaste.
> Praised be you, my Lord, through Brother Fire, through whom you light the night, and he is beautiful and playful and robust and strong.
> Praised be you my Lord, through our Sister Mother Earth, who sustains and governs us, and who produces various fruit with colored flowers and herbs. (CtC 5–9)

In addition to verses 1–9, Francis also composed a verse potentially used as a refrain, copied as the canticle's last verse: "Praise and Bless my Lord and give Him thanks and serve him with great humility" (CtC 14). One source relates that Francis imagined Brother Pacifico, a former master of singers, could go around with some brothers who would preach a sermon and then sing the canticle. When they were done, Francis thought the preacher should say, "We are *ioculatores Domini* [the Lord's jesters/players] and this is what we want as payment [for entertaining you]: that you live in true penance" (AC 83). Francis acted like a jester many times; vagabond entertainers he saw as a good likeness of "the servants of God…who must stir people's hearts and lift them up to spiritual joy" (AC 83). Perhaps he played the jester best at Greccio, where he set the scene of the nativity to stir the crowd's memory to renewed understanding of the Christmas mystery. The canticle sets a scene too, this time of Genesis and other biblical passages that sing of creation and its Creator. Francis's canticle may most closely relate to Daniel 3, the song of the three men in the furnace, which Francis prayed at least on Sundays as part of the Office and which he imitated in the praises of his Office of the Passion. Like those men, Francis turns his lips to praise from a furnace, the furnace of his own suffering, but for Francis there will be no angelic relief (Dan 3:49).

Although Francis's memory included the Scriptures in his canticle, he still sings as no Letters of Scripture do when he addresses created things as brothers and sisters. This form of address, at one level, expresses not unqualified reverence for creation but reverence for a creation who has a Father, reverence for the Creator God who gives life to these brothers and sisters (and mother), and reverence for the relationships among created things. Francis's reverence for the Creator through creation is well attested. One story tells, for instance, that Francis encouraged the friar tending a garden to leave a space where "Brother Flowers" could grow as wild as they pleased. "Thus, in their time they would invite all who saw the beautiful flowers to praise God, for every creature announces and proclaims, 'God made me for you, O human being.'" (AC 88). Thomas of Celano in his recently rediscovered *Life of Saint Francis* also observes in summary: "Indeed who is even able to speak of the sweetness that [Francis] enjoyed when contemplating in creatures the wisdom of the Creator, his power, and goodness?...On account of their single principle, he called all creatures by a fraternal name" (RL 65).

Francis revered creation as a gift of God that can aid us physically and spiritually when we attend to it. Francis also revered creation because of the exact ways that the Scriptures made reference to the created world. Thus, "Whenever [Francis] had to walk over rocks, he would walk with fear and reverence out of love for Him who is called 'The Rock'" (AC 88), a name for God in various biblical texts. Francis also picked up worms on the road and placed them safely off the path "because he had read what was said of the Savior, 'I am a worm, and not a man'" (Ps 22:7; RL 64). Stories of Francis ransoming "brother lamb" fit this same pattern. Francis reads creation through the Letters of Scripture and reveres certain parts of creation precisely because of who or what those things signify in the Scriptures (see 1C 77–79). Francis's love and care for the brothers and sisters of creation were, therefore, another way for him to embrace the Letter. Let us reflect on this further.

If created things are our brothers and sisters, then we may think of ourselves as the older siblings who have charge over them and who stand to gain the inheritance. If we think this way, perhaps we also wish to get the inheritance, and what power we think it offers, as soon as we can. But humanity,

created last in Genesis 1, is not the first among the siblings of
the earth but the last and the youngest. Humanity is therefore
last in line for the inheritance and needs the care of its older
siblings. But, like Joseph, our coming later and ultimately by
a different mother, is no sign that we are not wanted or lesser
but that we are loved and cherished and have in fact been
put in a providential role to care for all these siblings, even
Mother Earth, "who sustains and governs us." For the Word
of the Father formed our mother Earth who gives birth to our
temporal life, and that same Word formed our mother the
Church who gives us rebirth to eternal life through his suffering and death because he chose to empty himself for our
sakes. Francis, who always wishes to follow the Lord's footprints, renounces his claims to lordship over created things
because he desires to be subject to every creature for God's
sake (ER 16). Divested of power, Francis can use creation not
for mastery but for service, and the ultimate service is to give
God praise, which he does.

Francis met his bitter suffering and pain with music,
ordering the descent of his last days with sweet harmonies.
"Indeed, as his illness grew more serious, [Francis] himself
began to say the Canticle and afterwards had his companions sing it, so that in reflecting on the praise of the Lord, he
could forget the bitterness of his pains and illnesses. He did
this until the day of his death" (AC 83). But Francis's life was
not yet over, and his canticle was not yet finished. While still
at that hut next to San Damiano, Francis got news of con-
flict in Assisi. The bishop of Assisi had excommunicated the
podestà or "governor" of Assisi. The *podestà* in his turn publicly
demanded that no one engage in business with the bishop—
neither buying nor selling nor engaging in any contracts with
him (AC 84). It looked like the stalemate between the two
could last for a while, for the text bluntly tells us that the two
men "thoroughly hated each other" and that "there was no

one, religious or secular, who was intervening for peace and harmony between them" (AC 84). The Lord's jester decided to do what he could; he turned to song, and added verses 10–11 to his "Canticle of Brother Sun."

One source says that after Francis added this verse, he called one of his companions and told him: "Go to the *podestà* and, on my behalf, tell him to go to the bishop's residence together with the city's magistrates and bring with him as many others as he can." When the brother had gone, he said to two of his other companions: "Go and sing the *Canticle of Brother Sun* before the bishop, the *podestà*, and the others who are with them. I trust in the Lord that he will humble their hearts and they will make peace with each other and return to their earlier friendship and love" (AC 84).

The brothers did exactly as Francis asked, and the bishop and the *podestà* complied, demonstrating their mutual respect for Francis. All gathered at the bishop's residence. The two brothers then got up in front of everyone and said, working to capture the hearts of their audience, "In his illness, blessed Francis wrote the Praises of the Lord for his creatures, for His praise and the edification of neighbor. He asks you, then, to listen to them with great devotion" (AC 84). Perhaps some of those gathered had heard this canticle sung in Assisi before. They had not heard the new verse. As the brothers began to sing, the *podestà* immediately stood up and folded his arms and hands devoutly, as though he were listening to the Gospel, his eyes welling with tears out of respect for Francis (AC 84). Then the brothers came to the new verse and sang:

> Praised be You, my Lord, through those who give pardon for Your love, and bear infirmity and tribulation. Blessed are those who endure in peace for by You, Most High, shall they be crowned. (CtC 10–11)

The *podestà* was overcome. He cast himself at the bishop's feet, forgiving him. "Behold, I am ready to make amends to you for everything," the powerful man said in his tears, "as it pleases you, for the love of our Lord Jesus Christ and of his servant blessed Francis" (AC 84). The bishop reciprocated: "'Because of my office it is fitting that I be humble, but because I am naturally prone to anger, you must stoop to forgive me.' And so, with great kindness and love they embraced and kissed each other" (AC 84). That kiss was the medieval sign that all had indeed been forgiven. For in medieval law, disputes were settled by the drawing up of a contract between the offended parties that was then sealed with the embrace and kiss of the two parties.[1] Francis had provided the contract and his words provoked the kiss.

The brothers were amazed because what Francis "had foretold about peace and harmony between them had been fulfilled, to the letter [*ad litteram*]" (AC 84). Everyone else took it as a miracle too, enabled by Francis's intercession, that the matter had been resolved so quickly "and that without recalling anything that had been said, they returned to such harmony from such scandal" (AC 84). At Greccio, Francis had played the jester himself and renewed the memories of those in attendance by giving them a new vision of the familiar Letter. Now the brothers had to play the jester for him. His words were just as effective because Francis healed by crafting from the Letter with the Spirit. He proposed peace and forgiveness in terms recalling the Gospel, the Beatitudes, and Christ's cross, which is our peace. "May the Lord give you his peace" was the greeting the Lord had revealed to Francis; that peace he and his brothers announced as they traveled; that peace he surely sought in the hovel next to San

---

1. For more on peacemaking in the Middle Ages and this episode of Francis making peace, see Katherine Jansen, *Peace and Penance in Late Medieval Italy* (Princeton, NJ: Princeton University Press, 2018).

Damiano. Thus, a new verse came into being and became a permanent part of the canticle. Francis's song, however, was not yet finished.

At some point, as his illness worsened, Francis asked the brothers to move him to St. Mary of the Angels, the Portiuncula, the "mother-church" of the Order of Lesser Brothers. He knew that his stay would not be long. Before the move, a doctor came to see Francis. The doctor feared to tell Francis the truth about his illnesses, but Francis coaxed it out of him, assuring the doctor that he was not a coward (a *corculus*— small-hearted) who feared death. So, the doctor told him plainly: "Your illness is incurable, and you will die either at the end of September or on the fourth day before the Nones of October" (*AC* 100), meaning October 4. Francis stretched out his arms to the Lord and said with joy, "Welcome, my sister death" (*AC* 100).

Before that sister arrived, Francis still hoped to be with those he loved. In particular was a woman named Lady Jacoba, a pious widow from one of the noble families of Rome. Francis ordered a brother to deliver a letter to Jacoba asking her to come see him soon. Francis wanted her to bring cloth for a habit and ingredients for a confection of nuts and honey he liked called *mostacciolo*, which Jacoba had previously made for Francis when he visited Rome. Just as the brother was dispatched, a knock came at the door; it was Lady Jacoba with her son and various other people from Rome. Jacoba explained to the confused brothers that in prayer she had been told to hurry to Francis and to bring cloth, makings for mostacciolo, incense, and wax for candles. Now that she was here, the brothers had a different problem. Could they let Jacoba in? Francis himself had ordered that women could not be present in the brothers' quarters. Paying attention to what was right before him, Francis said, "This command need not be observed in the case of this lady whose faith and devotion made her come here from so far away" (*AC* 8). Jacoba wept as she entered, while the brothers stood amazed that she had come with the very things Francis had wanted and more besides. The cloth Jacoba brought they turned into his burial garment, appropriately patched so that it still seemed "poor." Jacoba made Francis mostacciolo later in the week, a sweetness for his passage, but he could hardly eat any of it (*AC* 8).

Sister Death hastened. Francis kept at the Letter. He prayed the Office or had a brother say it in his presence. When he thought that the end was very close, he asked to be placed on the ground naked. His brothers complied. Looking at their faces, he said to them, "I have done what is mine, may Christ teach you what is yours" (2C 162). The brothers wept. The brother assigned as Francis's guardian then ordered Francis under obedience (the only way to get him to do it) to accept the new tunic that he would be buried in, the one made from Lady Jacoba's cloth. The guardian made sure to say that Francis had no authority to give it away to anyone else, since the tunic did not belong to him at all but was only being lent to him (2C 162). Francis accepted the new tunic happily, for in accepting it he remained poor and obedient. Looking at the brothers around him, he blessed them, like a dying patriarch. He asked for bread, blessed it, broke it with his weary hands, or had another brother break it, and gave everyone a piece to eat (2C 163; *AC* 22). He called for the Book of the Gospels and asked a brother to start reading at John 13:1. Thomas of Celano explains what is perhaps obvious to us: "He was remembering that most sacred Supper, the last one the Lord celebrated with his disciples. In reverent memory of this, to show his brothers how much he loved them, he did all of this" (2C 163). He was too sick to wash their feet, so he put their minds awash in the Lord's memory, whose footprints he and they had promised to follow.

At some point in the night, he suddenly broke into a psalm (142): "With a loud voice I cried to the Lord. With my voice I beseeched the Lord." Then, before he died, perhaps right in his very final moments, he sang for a last time his new canticle. During those final days of his life, surrounded by the Letter and the brothers and sisters who loved it, he again added new verses to his canticle. Attentive to what was happening to him and to those who loved him, attentive to his body and soul, attentive to the song and the praises he wished to make, he called for Brother Angelo and Brother Leo so that they could sing to him of Sister Death (AC 7). He gave them the words that finished his canticle:

Praised be you my Lord through our Sister Bodily Death, from whom no one living can escape. Woe to those who die in mortal sin. Blessed are those whom death will find in Your most holy will, for the second death shall do them no harm. (CtC 12–13)

These last footprints of the Lord, the footprints of suffering and death, these too Francis would step into and praise. He sang an admonition to himself as he died and to all who heard the song: the only death to fear is the death of sin. For "we know that he [the Lord] is coming, that he will come to judge justice" (OfP 6). Sister Death brings us all to that judgment, the same Sister to whom our Lord was obedient. Only sin could make the Lord's footprints bitter to follow, for even death's bitterness has been made a sweetness by the one who died for us and left us a memorial of his death and resurrection, a sweetness for our passage: himself and his words.

7

Bearing Over/*Translatio*

A rush of wings broke the doleful silence of those around the body of Francis. The brothers had laid him out upon the ground, as he had asked, a last gesture of humility, a word rooted in the Latin word *humus*, meaning "earth" or "ground." Now in this night of passing, came the larks, birds of the morning. That is what the stories say. The larks came and landed and sang as Francis died. Their brother, a philomena, had sung his last Office, sung until he could not, sung for love of him who died for love of us, and the larks came despite their nature to announce a dawn in the dark of night.

Bells rang out. A crowd from Assisi descended to see the body of Francis. The grieving brothers played host through their tears. Waves of sorrow beat upon them. They had lost their father and brother. But as they wept, another wave began to crest. Sister Death revealed Francis as he was. He could no longer hide the stigmata, the Letter traced in his flesh, the Letter the Spirit had made of him on La Verna.

Thomas of Celano was there that night. He did not know what he was about to see when he beheld Francis's body. Stunned by what he saw, he must have sought out what had happened, and so learned the story of La Verna. Thomas seems wrapped in a vision when he writes of the sight of Francis's body. He sees in Francis and the stigmata "signs of martyrdom that do not inflict horror on the minds of those who see them but grant much beauty and grace." Francis's body in death displayed "a miracle worthy of ever-lasting remembrance and a sacrament to be remembered," a sign of the "sublime splendor of the living cross, giving life to the dead" (1C 113, 114). "He had," Thomas writes, "both the image and the form of the Seraph" (1C 115), for Francis had become a man full of praise, even in his suffering, because he held to the memory of the one who asked us to "do this in memory of me."

In the morning, after keeping vigil in the night, the brothers took up the dead body of Francis, scarred and bro-ken and speaking glory, and walked to San Damiano (1C 116–17). The poor church had a little window through which the sisters received the body of Christ from their quarters. Through that same window they now saw and touched the body of Francis. Clare grieved for this friend and brother, this father, whom she had once understood in a vision to have nourished her on the Gospel itself, whose body in that vision had become a mirror (PC in CA:ED, 161). The broth-ers held that bright mirror up to the window for her to wash in tears. Clare remained at San Damiano for nearly thirty more years, living the Letter boldly with her sisters.

Onward the brothers walked, bearing Francis's body. Up the hill where once he raced to get stones, they carried the one who had become a living stone (1 Pet 2:5). They came to the Church of St. George and entombed his body. Miracles soon flowed from the place. It was October 4, 1226. Four years later, on May 25, the brothers moved Fran-cis's body again to the newly constructed but not yet deco-rated Basilica of St. Francis in Assisi. The day became a feast of its own—the feast of Francis's *translatio*, a celebration of the movement of his body from one church to another. The Church of St. George would eventually become the Basilica of St. Clare, where her body still lies. Cimabue and Giotto, among other great artists, adorned the Basilica of St. Francis with their talent and insight, making it one of the most beautiful churches in the world and Assisi a destination for many pilgrims. Though steeped in war and feuds like most medieval cities, Assisi has become a place of surpassing peace, a peace every pilgrim lauds so much that one wonders if it is real. I was a pilgrim at Assisi and La Verna once too. It was not a pilgrimage I had planned or sought. I went with a companion I barely knew, whose generosity I cannot forget. I tell you: the pilgrims do not lie.

In gardens, many people keep a reminder of Francis, a statue of a peaceful man, often with a modest smile, birds atop his shoulders, a book in his hands. Through this simple image, Francis is calling us to the Letter. He calls us to the Letter of creation, to see in its mirror with the Spirit's aid the Lord who created all things great and small, for whom Francis gladly became a fool, to preach the Letter to every creature under heaven (Col 1:23). He calls us to the Letter of Scripture, a lamp for our feet and a light for our path (Ps 119:105), to pray in the Spirit with the word that saturated his mind like spring rain on bare earth. He calls us to the Letter of worship, to the place where the Lord's words and the Spirit bring the Lord himself into our midst, where we feed on him, and he makes us one. This unity with Christ is the peace of the Lord—the peace that Francis preached in churches and city squares, that he announced to strangers on muddy roads, that he groaned for on clear mountain tops. He received that peace in odd places—in city streets and lepers' homes, in forgotten churches with old crosses, in the company of unexpected brothers and sisters, on a cold mountain top. That peace is not always light and airy, not always accompanied by laughter and joy; that peace can be heavy, that peace can be made of wounds and dirt.

We chase after the peace that new things might bring, but there is only one who can say "See, I am making all things new" (Rev 21:5). He made all things new on Golgotha, but we groan in anticipation of its fulfillment. He displays that newness on our altars, when with the Lord's own words, the Spirit comes, and bread and wine become his body and blood. Hearing his voice in the Scriptures, coming to his altar, we see that our transformation is not far off but near at hand, when, with the Spirit's sight, we confess the mystery and allow the Spirit to receive the Lord within us. What the Lord will do is new. The body the Lord is making is new. That new life is made by him who gave his life for us, who loved us to the end. Let us offer ourselves totally to him, who offers himself totally to us. He is making us a holy people. We shall bleed, we shall be wounded, our hearts shall be pierced through, for we are not angels. The victory is won, and we must let it take place in our body and soul, a victory marked not with medals and banners but with the wounds of Christ. Rejoice! Soon, very soon, the trumpet shall sound, and every tear shall be wiped away, and the sun and moon surpassed, for the very Lamb upon our altars shall himself be our light (Rev 21:23).